AN ENEMY OF THE PEOPLE

INSIGHT PUBLICA®

Nadakkavu, Kozhikode, Kerala, 673011
www.insightpublica.com
e-mail: insightpublica@gmail.com
Title: An Enemy of the People
Author: Henrik Ibsen
Translator: R. Farquharson Sharp
First Insight Edition: March 2023
Layout&Cover: kjvj@insight

Printed and Published by
InsightinPublica Printers & Publishers Pvt. Ltd.
ISBN 978-93-5517-175-7

AN ENEMY OF THE PEOPLE

A play in five acts

by

Henrik Ibsen

Translated by R. Farquharson Sharp

INSIGHT PUBLICA

DRAMATIS PERSONAE

Dr. Thomas Stockmann, Medical Officer of the Municipal Baths.

Mrs. Stockmann, his wife.

Petra (their daughter) a teacher.

Ejlif & Morten (their sons, aged 13 and 10 respectively).

Peter Stockmann (the Doctor's elder brother), Mayor of the

Town and Chief Constable, Chairman of the Baths' Committee, etc.

Morten Kiil, a tanner (Mrs. Stockmann's adoptive father).

Hovstad, editor of the "People's Messenger."

Billing, sub-editor.

Captain Horster.

Aslaksen, a printer.

Men of various conditions and occupations, a few women, and a troop of schoolboys—the audience at a public meeting.

The action takes place in a coastal town in southern Norway,

Henrik Johan Ibsen (20 March 1828 – 23 May 1906) was a Norwegian playwright and theatre director. As one of the founders of modernism in theatre, Ibsen is often referred to as “the father of realism” and one of the most influential playwrights of his time.

ACT I

(SCENE.—DR. STOCKMANN'S sitting-room. It is evening. The room is plainly but neatly appointed and furnished. In the right-hand wall are two doors; the farther leads out to the hall, the nearer to the doctor's study. In the left-hand wall, opposite the door leading to the hall, is a door leading to the other rooms occupied by the family. In the middle of the same wall stands the stove, and, further forward, a couch with a looking-glass hanging over it and an oval table in front of it. On the table, a lighted lamp, with a lampshade. At the back of the room, an open door leads to the dining-room. BILLING is seen sitting at the dining table, on which a lamp is burning. He has a napkin tucked under his chin, and MRS. STOCKMANN is standing by the table handing him a large plate-full of roast beef. The other places at the table are empty, and the table somewhat in disorder, evidently a meal having recently been finished.)

Mrs. Stockmann. You see, if you come an hour late, Mr. Billing, you have to put up with cold meat.

Billing (as he eats). It is uncommonly good, thank you—remarkably good.

Mrs. Stockmann. My husband makes such a point of having his meals punctually, you know.

Billing. That doesn't affect me a bit. Indeed, I almost think I enjoy a meal all the better when I can sit down and eat all by myself, and undisturbed.

Mrs. Stockmann. Oh well, as long as you are enjoying it—. (Turns to the hall door, listening.) I expect that is Mr. Hovstad coming too.

Billing. Very likely.

(PETER STOCKMANN comes in. He wears an overcoat and his official hat, and carries a stick.)

Peter Stockmann. Good evening, Katherine.

Mrs. Stockmann (coming forward into the sitting-room). Ah, good evening—is it you? How good of you to come up and see us!

Peter Stockmann. I happened to be passing, and so—(looks into the dining-room). But you have company with you, I see.

Mrs. Stockmann (a little embarrassed). Oh, no—it was quite by chance he came in. (Hurriedly.) Won't you come in and have something, too?

Peter Stockmann. I! No, thank you. Good gracious—hot meat at night! Not with my digestion.

Mrs. Stockmann. Oh, but just once in a way—

Peter Stockmann. No, no, my dear lady; I stick to my tea and bread and butter. It is much more wholesome in the long run—and a little more economical, too.

Mrs. Stockmann (smiling). Now you mustn't think that Thomas and I are spendthrifts.

Peter Stockmann. Not you, my dear; I would never think that of you. (Points to the Doctor's study.) Is he not at home?

Mrs. Stockmann. No, he went out for a little turn after supper—he and the boys.

Peter Stockmann. I doubt if that is a wise thing to do. (Listens.) I fancy I hear him coming now.

Mrs. Stockmann. No, I don't think it is he. (A knock is heard at the door.) Come in! (HOVSTAD comes in from the hall.) Oh, it is you, Mr. Hovstad!

Hovstad. Yes, I hope you will forgive me, but I was delayed at the printers. Good evening, Mr. Mayor.

Peter Stockmann (bowing a little distantly). Good evening. You have come on business, no doubt.

Hovstad. Partly. It's about an article for the paper.

Peter Stockmann. So I imagined. I hear my brother has become a prolific contributor to the "People's Messenger."

Hovstad. Yes, he is good enough to write in the "People's Messenger" when he has any home truths to tell.

Mrs. Stockmann (to HOVSTAD). But won't you—? (Points to the dining-room.)

Peter Stockmann. Quite so, quite so. I don't blame him in the least, as a writer, for addressing himself to the quarters where he will find the readiest sympathy. And, besides that, I personally have no reason to bear any ill will to your paper, Mr. Hovstad.

Hovstad. I quite agree with you.

Peter Stockmann. Taking one thing with another, there is an excellent spirit of toleration in the town—an admirable municipal spirit. And it all springs from the fact of our having a great common interest to unite us—an interest that is in an equally high degree the concern of every right-minded Citizen.

Hovstad. The Baths, yes.

Peter Stockmann. Exactly—-our fine, new, handsome Baths. Mark my words, Mr. Hovstad—the Baths will become the focus of our municipal life! Not a doubt of it!

Mrs. Stockmann. That is just what Thomas says.

Peter Stockmann. Think how extraordinarily the place has developed within the last year or two! Money has been flowing in, and there is some life and some business doing in the town. Houses and landed property are rising in value every day.

Hovstad. And unemployment is diminishing,

Peter Stockmann. Yes, that is another thing. The burden on the poor rates has been lightened, to the great relief of the propertied classes; and that relief will be even greater if only we get a really good summer this year, and lots of visitors—plenty of invalids, who will make the Baths talked about.

Hovstad. And there is a good prospect of that, I hear.

Peter Stockmann. It looks very promising. Inquiries about apartments and that sort of thing are reaching us, every day.

Hovstad. Well, the doctor's article will come in very suitably.

Peter Stockmann. Has he been writing something just lately?

Hovstad. This is something he wrote in the winter; a recommendation of the Baths—an account of the excellent sanitary conditions here. But I held the article over, temporarily.

Peter Stockmann. Ah,—some little difficulty about it, I suppose?

Hovstad. No, not at all; I thought it would be better to wait until the spring, because it is just at this time that people begin to think seriously about their summer quarters.

Peter Stockmann. Quite right; you were perfectly right, Mr. Hovstad.

Hovstad. Yes, Thomas is really indefatigable when it is a question of the Baths.

Peter Stockmann. Well remember, he is the Medical Officer to the Baths.

Hovstad. Yes, and what is more, they owe their existence to him.

Peter Stockmann. To him? Indeed! It is true I have heard from time to time that some people are of that opinion. At the same time I must say I imagined that I took a modest part in the enterprise.

Mrs. Stockmann. Yes, that is what Thomas is always saying.

Hovstad. But who denies it, Mr. Stockmann? You set the thing going and made a practical concern of it; we all know that. I only meant that the idea of it came first from the doctor.

Peter Stockmann. Oh, ideas yes! My brother has had plenty of them in his time—unfortunately. But when it is a question of putting an idea into practical shape, you have to apply to a man of different mettle, Mr. Hovstad. And I certainly should have thought that in this house at least...

Mrs. Stockmann. My dear Peter—

Hovstad. How can you think that—?

Mrs. Stockmann. Won't you go in and have something, Mr. Hovstad? My husband is sure to be back directly.

Hovstad. Thank you, perhaps just a morsel. (Goes into the dining-room.)

Peter Stockmann (lowering his voice a little). It is a curious thing that these farmers' sons never seem to lose their want of tact.

Mrs. Stockmann. Surely it is not worth bothering about! Cannot you and Thomas share the credit as brothers?

Peter Stockmann. I should have thought so; but apparently some people are not satisfied with a share.

Mrs. Stockmann. What nonsense! You and Thomas get on so capitally together. (Listens.) There he is at last, I think. (Goes out and opens the door leading to the hall.)

Dr. Stockmann (laughing and talking outside). Look here—here is another guest for you, Katherine. Isn't that jolly! Come in, Captain Horster; hang your coat up on this peg. Ah, you don't wear an overcoat. Just think, Katherine; I met him in the street and could hardly persuade him to come up! (CAPTAIN HORSTER comes into the room and greets MRS. STOCKMANN. He is followed by Dr. Stockmann.) Come along in, boys. They are ravenously hungry again, you know. Come along, Captain Horster; you must have a slice of beef. (Pushes HORSTER into the dining-room. EJLIF and MORTEN go in after them.)

Mrs. Stockmann. But, Thomas, don't you see—?

Dr. Stockmann (turning in the doorway). Oh, is it you, Peter? (Shakes hands with him.) Now that is very delightful.

Peter Stockmann. Unfortunately I must go in a moment—

Dr. Stockmann. Rubbish! There is some toddy just coming in. You haven't forgotten the toddy, Katherine?

Mrs. Stockmann. Of course not; the water is boiling now. (Goes into the dining-room.)

Peter Stockmann. Toddy too!

Dr. Stockmann. Yes, sit down and we will have it comfortably.

Peter Stockmann. Thanks, I never care about an evening's drinking.

Dr. Stockmann. But this isn't an evening's drinking.

Peter Stockmann. It seems to me—. (Looks towards the dining-room.) It is extraordinary how they can put away all that food.

Dr. Stockmann (rubbing his hands). Yes, isn't it splendid to see young people eat? They have always got an appetite, you know! That's as it should be.

Lots of food—to build up their strength! They are the people who are going to stir up the fermenting forces of the future, Peter.

Peter Stockmann. May I ask what they will find here to "stir up," as you put it?

Dr. Stockmann. Ah, you must ask the young people that—when the times comes. We shan't be able to see it, of course. That stands to reason—two old fogies, like us.

Peter Stockmann. Really, really! I must say that is an extremely odd expression to—

Dr. Stockmann. Oh, you mustn't take me too literally, Peter. I am so heartily happy and contented, you know. I think it is such an extraordinary piece of good fortune to be in the middle of all this growing, germinating life. It is a splendid time to live in! It is as if a whole new world were being created around one.

Peter Stockmann. Do you really think so?

Dr. Stockmann. Ah, naturally you can't appreciate it as keenly as I. You have lived all your life in these surroundings, and your impressions have been blunted. But I, who have been buried all these years in my little corner up north, almost without ever seeing a stranger who might bring new ideas with him—well, in my case it has just the same effect as if I had been transported into the middle of a crowded city.

Peter Stockmann. Oh, a city—!

Dr. Stockmann. I know, I know; it is all cramped enough here, compared with many other places. But there is life here—there is promise—there are innumerable things to work for and fight for; and that is the main thing. (Calls.) Katherine, hasn't the postman been here?

Mrs. Stockmann (from the dining-room). No.

Dr. Stockmann. And then to be comfortably off, Peter! That is something one learns to value, when one has been on the brink of starvation, as we have.

Peter Stockmann. Oh, surely—

Dr. Stockmann. Indeed I can assure you we have often been very hard put to it, up there. And now to be able to live like a lord! Today, for instance, we had roast beef for dinner—and, what is more, for supper too. Won't you come and have a little bit? Or let me show it you, at any rate? Come here—

Peter Stockmann. No, no—not for worlds!

Dr. Stockmann. Well, but just come here then. Do you see, we have got a table-cover?

Peter Stockmann. Yes, I noticed it.

Dr. Stockmann. And we have got a lamp-shade too. Do you see? All out of Katherine's savings! It makes the room so cosy. Don't you think so? Just stand here for a moment—no, no, not there—just here, that's it! Look now, when you get the light on it altogether. I really think it looks very nice, doesn't it?

Peter Stockmann. Oh, if you can afford luxuries of this kind—

Dr. Stockmann. Yes, I can afford it now. Katherine tells me I earn almost as much as we spend.

Peter Stockmann. Almost—yes!

Dr. Stockmann. But a scientific man must live in a little bit of style. I am quite sure an ordinary civil servant spends more in a year than I do.

Peter Stockmann. I daresay. A civil servant—a man in a well-paid position...

Dr. Stockmann. Well, any ordinary merchant, then! A man in that position spends two or three times as much as—

Peter Stockmann. It just depends on circumstances.

Dr. Stockmann. At all events I assure you I don't waste money unprofitably. But I can't find it in my heart to deny myself the pleasure of entertaining my friends. I need that sort of thing, you know. I have lived for so long shut out of it all, that it is a necessity of life to me to mix with young, eager, ambitious men, men of liberal and active minds; and that describes every one of those fellows who are enjoying their supper in there. I wish you knew more of Hovstad.

Peter Stockmann. By the way, Hovstad was telling me he was going to print another article of yours.

Dr. Stockmann. An article of mine?

Peter Stockmann. Yes, about the Baths. An article you wrote in the winter.

Dr. Stockmann. Oh, that one! No, I don't intend that to appear just for the present.

Peter Stockmann. Why not? It seems to me that this would be the most opportune moment.

Dr. Stockmann. Yes, very likely—under normal conditions. (Crosses the room.)

Peter Stockmann (following him with his eyes). Is there anything abnormal about the present conditions?

Dr. Stockmann (standing still). To tell you the truth, Peter, I can't say just at this moment—at all events not tonight. There may be much that is very abnormal about the present conditions—and it is possible there may be nothing abnormal about them at all. It is quite possible it may be merely my imagination.

Peter Stockmann. I must say it all sounds most mysterious. Is there something going on that I am to be kept in ignorance of? I should have imagined that I, as Chairman of the governing body of the Baths—

Dr. Stockmann. And I should have imagined that I—. Oh, come, don't let us fly out at one another, Peter.

Peter Stockmann. Heaven forbid! I am not in the habit of flying out at people, as you call it. But I am entitled to request most emphatically that all arrangements shall be made in a businesslike manner, through the proper channels, and shall be dealt with by the legally constituted authorities. I can allow no going behind our backs by any roundabout means.

Dr. Stockmann. Have I ever at any time tried to go behind your backs?

Peter Stockmann. You have an ingrained tendency to take your own way, at all events; and, that is almost equally inadmissible in a well ordered community. The individual ought undoubtedly to acquiesce in subordinating himself to the community—or, to speak more accurately, to the authorities who have the care of the community's welfare.

Dr. Stockmann. Very likely. But what the deuce has all this got to do with me?

Peter Stockmann. That is exactly what you never appear to be willing to learn, my dear Thomas. But, mark my words, some day you will have to suffer for it—sooner or later. Now I have told you. Good-bye.

Dr. Stockmann. Have you taken leave of your senses? You are on the wrong scent altogether.

Peter Stockmann. I am not usually that. You must excuse me now if I— (calls into the dining-room). Good night, Katherine. Good night, gentlemen. (Goes out.)

Mrs. Stockmann (coming from the dining-room). Has he gone?

Dr. Stockmann. Yes, and in such a bad temper.

Mrs. Stockmann. But, dear Thomas, what have you been doing to him again?

Dr. Stockmann. Nothing at all. And, anyhow, he can't oblige me to make my report before the proper time.

Mrs. Stockmann. What have you got to make a report to him about?

Dr. Stockmann. Hm! Leave that to me, Katherine. It is an extraordinary thing that the postman doesn't come.

(HOVSTAD, BILLING and HORSTER have got up from the table and come into the sitting-room. EJLIF and MORTEN come in after them.)

Billing (stretching himself). Ah!—one feels a new man after a meal like that.

Hovstad. The mayor wasn't in a very sweet temper tonight, then.

Dr. Stockmann. It is his stomach; he has wretched digestion.

Hovstad. I rather think it was us two of the "People's Messenger" that he couldn't digest.

Mrs. Stockmann. I thought you came out of it pretty well with him.

Hovstad. Oh yes; but it isn't anything more than a sort of truce.

Billing. That is just what it is! That word sums up the situation.

Dr. Stockmann. We must remember that Peter is a lonely man, poor chap. He has no home comforts of any kind; nothing but everlasting business. And all that infernal weak tea wash that he pours into himself! Now then, my boys, bring chairs up to the table. Aren't we going to have that toddy, Katherine?

Mrs. Stockmann (going into the dining-room). I am just getting it.

Dr. Stockmann. Sit down here on the couch beside me, Captain Horster. We so seldom see you. Please sit down, my friends. (They sit down at the table. MRS. STOCKMANN brings a tray, with a spirit-lamp, glasses, bottles, etc., upon it.)

Mrs. Stockmann. There you are! This is arrack, and this is rum, and this one is the brandy. Now every one must help themselves.

Dr. Stockmann (taking a glass). We will. (They all mix themselves some toddy.) And let us have the cigars. Ejlif, you know where the box is. And you, Morten, can fetch my pipe. (The two boys go into the room on the right.) I have a suspicion that Ejlif pockets a cigar now and then!—but I take no notice of it. (Calls out.) And my smoking-cap too, Morten. Katherine, you can tell him where I left it. Ah, he has got it. (The boys bring the various things.) Now, my friends. I stick to my pipe, you know. This one has seen plenty of bad weather with me up north. (Touches glasses with them.) Your good health! Ah, it is good to be sitting snug and warm here.

Mrs. Stockmann (who sits knitting). Do you sail soon, Captain Horster?

Horster. I expect to be ready to sail next week.

Mrs. Stockmann. I suppose you are going to America?

Horster. Yes, that is the plan.

Mrs. Stockmann. Then you won't be able to take part in the coming election?

Horster. Is there going to be an election?

Billing. Didn't you know?

Horster. No, I don't mix myself up with those things.

Billing. But do you not take an interest in public affairs?

Horster. No, I don't know anything about politics.

Billing.	All the same, one ought to vote, at any rate.
Horster.	Even if one doesn't know anything about what is going on?
Billing.	Doesn't know! What do you mean by that? A community is like a ship; everyone ought to be prepared to take the helm.
Horster.	Maybe that is all very well on shore; but on board ship it wouldn't work.
Hovstad.	It is astonishing how little most sailors care about what goes on on shore.
Billing.	Very extraordinary.
Dr. Stockmann.	Sailors are like birds of passage; they feel equally at home in any latitude. And that is only an additional reason for our being all the more keen, Hovstad. Is there to be anything of public interest in tomorrow's "Messenger"?
Hovstad.	Nothing about municipal affairs. But the day after tomorrow I was thinking of printing your article—
Dr. Stockmann.	Ah, devil take it—my article! Look here, that must wait a bit.
Hovstad.	Really? We had just got convenient space for it, and I thought it was just the opportune moment—
Dr. Stockmann.	Yes, yes, very likely you are right; but it must wait all the same. I will explain to you later. (PETRA comes in from the hall, in hat and cloak and with a bundle of exercise books under her arm.)
Petra.	Good evening.
Dr. Stockmann.	Good evening, Petra; come along.

(Mutual greetings; PETRA takes off her things and puts them down on a chair by the door.)

Petra.	And you have all been sitting here enjoying yourselves, while I have been out slaving!

Dr. Stockmann. Well, come and enjoy yourself too!

Billing. May I mix a glass for you?

Petra (coming to the table). Thanks, I would rather do it; you always mix it too strong. But I forgot, father—I have a letter for you. (Goes to the chair where she has laid her things.)

Dr. Stockmann. A letter? From whom?

Petra (looking in her coat pocket). The postman gave it to me just as I was going out.

Dr. Stockmann (getting up and going to her). And you only give to me now!

Petra. I really had not time to run up again. There it is!

Dr. Stockmann (seizing the letter). Let's see, let's see, child! (Looks at the address.) Yes, that's all right!

Mrs. Stockmann. Is it the one you have been expecting go anxiously, Thomas?

Dr. Stockmann. Yes, it is. I must go to my room now and— Where shall I get a light, Katherine? Is there no lamp in my room again?

Mrs. Stockmann. Yes, your lamp is already lit on your desk.

Dr. Stockmann. Good, good. Excuse me for a moment—, (Goes into his study.)

Petra. What do you suppose it is, mother?

Mrs. Stockmann. I don't know; for the last day or two he has always been asking if the postman has not been.

Billing. Probably some country patient.

Petra. Poor old dad!—he will overwork himself soon. (Mixes a glass for herself.) There, that will taste good!

Hovstad. Have you been teaching in the evening school again today?

Petra (sipping from her glass). Two hours.

Billing. And four hours of school in the morning?

Petra. Five hours.

Mrs. Stockmann. And you have still got exercises to correct, I see.

Petra. A whole heap, yes.

Horster. You are pretty full up with work too, it seems to me.

Petra. Yes—but that is good. One is so delightfully tired after it.

Billing. Do you like that?

Petra. Yes, because one sleeps so well then.

Morten. You must be dreadfully wicked, Petra.

Petra. Wicked?

Morten. Yes, because you work so much. Mr. Rorlund says work is a punishment for our sins.

Ejlif. Pooh, what a duffer, you are, to believe a thing like that!

Mrs. Stockmann. Come, come, Ejlif!

Billing (laughing). That's capital!

Hovstad. Don't you want to work as hard as that, Morten?

Morten. No, indeed I don't.

Hovstad. What do you want to be, then?

Morten. I should like best to be a Viking,

Ejlif. You would have to be a pagan then.

Morten. Well, I could become a pagan, couldn't I?

Billing. I agree with you, Morten! My sentiments, exactly.

Mrs. Stockmann (signalling to him). I am sure that is not true, Mr. Billing.

Billing. Yes, I swear it is! I am a pagan, and I am proud of it. Believe me, before long we shall all be pagans.

Morten. And then shall be allowed to do anything

we like?

Billing. Well, you'll see, Morten.

Mrs. Stockmann. You must go to your room now, boys; I am sure you have some lessons to learn for tomorrow.

Ejlif. I should like so much to stay a little longer—

Mrs. Stockmann. No, no; away you go, both of you, (The boys say good night and go into the room on the left.)

Hovstad. Do you really think it can do the boys any harm to hear such things?

Mrs. Stockmann. I don't know; but I don't like it.

Petra. But you know, mother, I think you really are wrong about it.

Mrs. Stockmann. Maybe, but I don't like it—not in our own home.

Petra. There is so much falsehood both at home and at school. At home one must not speak, and at school we have to stand and tell lies to the children.

Horster. Tell lies?

Petra. Yes, don't you suppose we have to teach them all sorts of things that we don't believe?

Billing. That is perfectly true.

Petra. If only I had the means, I would start a school of my own; and it would be conducted on very different lines.

Billing. Oh, bother the means—!

Horster. Well if you are thinking of that, Miss Stockmann, I shall be delighted to provide you with a schoolroom. The great big old house my father left me is standing almost empty; there is an immense dining-room downstairs—

Petra (laughing). Thank you very much; but I am afraid nothing will come of it.

Hovstad. No, Miss Petra is much more likely to take to journalism, I expect. By the way, have you had time to do anything with that English story you promised to translate for us?

Petra. No, not yet, but you shall have it in good time.

(DR. STOCKMANN comes in from his room with an open letter in his hand.)

Dr. Stockmann (waving the letter). Well, now the town will have something new to talk about, I can tell you!

Billing. Something new?

Mrs. Stockmann. What is this?

Dr. Stockmann. A great discovery, Katherine.

Hovstad. Really?

Mrs. Stockmann. A discovery of yours?

Dr. Stockmann. A discovery of mine. (Walks up and down.) Just let them come saying, as usual, that it is all fancy and a crazy man's imagination! But they will be careful what they say this time, I can tell you!

Petra. But, father, tell us what it is.

Dr. Stockmann. Yes, yes—only give me time, and you shall know all about it. If only I had Peter here now! It just shows how we men can go about forming our judgments, when in reality we are as blind as any moles—

Hovstad. What are you driving at, Doctor?

Dr. Stockmann (standing still by the table). Isn't it the universal opinion that our town is a healthy spot?

Hovstad. Certainly.

Dr. Stockmann. Quite an unusually healthy spot, in fact—a place that deserves to be recommended in the warmest possible manner either for invalids or for people who are well—

Mrs. Stockmann. Yes, but my dear Thomas—

Dr. Stockmann. And we have been recommending it and praising it—I have written and written, both in the "Messenger" and in pamphlets...

Hovstad. Well, what then?

Dr. Stockmann. And the Baths—we have called them the "main artery of the town's life-blood," the "nerve-centre of our town," and the devil knows what else—

Billing. "The town's pulsating heart" was the expression I once used on an important occasion.

Dr. Stockmann. Quite so. Well, do you know what they really are, these great, splendid, much praised Baths, that have cost so much money—do you know what they are?

Hovstad. No, what are they?

Mrs. Stockmann. Yes, what are they?

Dr. Stockmann. The whole place is a pest-house!

Petra. The Baths, father?

Mrs. Stockmann (at the same time), Our Baths?

Hovstad. But, Doctor—

Billing. Absolutely incredible!

Dr. Stockmann. The whole Bath establishment is a whited, poisoned sepulchre, I tell you—the gravest possible danger to the public health! All the nastiness up at Molledal, all that stinking filth, is infecting the water in the conduit-pipes leading to the reservoir; and the same cursed, filthy poison oozes out on the shore too—

Horster. Where the bathing-place is?

Dr. Stockmann. Just there.

Hovstad. How do you come to be so certain of all

this, Doctor?

Dr. Stockmann. I have investigated the matter most conscientiously. For a long time past I have suspected something of the kind. Last year we had some very strange cases of illness among the visitors—typhoid cases, and cases of gastric fever—

Mrs. Stockmann. Yes, that is quite true.

Dr. Stockmann. At the time, we supposed the visitors had been infected before they came; but later on, in the winter, I began to have a different opinion; and so I set myself to examine the water, as well as I could.

Mrs. Stockmann. Then that is what you have been so busy with?

Dr. Stockmann. Indeed I have been busy, Katherine. But here I had none of the necessary scientific apparatus; so I sent samples, both of the drinking-water and of the sea-water, up to the University, to have an accurate analysis made by a chemist.

Hovstad. And have you got that?

Dr. Stockmann (showing him the letter). Here it is! It proves the presence of decomposing organic matter in the water—it is full of infusoria. The water is absolutely dangerous to use, either internally or externally.

Mrs. Stockmann. What a mercy you discovered it in time.

Dr. Stockmann. You may well say so.

Hovstad. And what do you propose to do now, Doctor?

Dr. Stockmann. To see the matter put right, naturally.

Hovstad. Can that be done?

Dr. Stockmann. It must be done. Otherwise the Baths will be absolutely useless and wasted. But we need not anticipate that; I have a very clear idea what we shall have to do.

Mrs. Stockmann. But why have you kept this all so secret, dear?

Dr. Stockmann. Do you suppose I was going to run about the town gossiping about it, before I had absolute proof? No, thank you. I am not such a fool.

Petra. Still, you might have told us—

Dr. Stockmann. Not a living soul. But tomorrow you may run around to the old Badger—

Mrs. Stockmann. Oh, Thomas! Thomas!

Dr. Stockmann. Well, to your grandfather, then. The old boy will have something to be astonished at! I know he thinks I am cracked—and there are lots of other people who think so too, I have noticed. But now these good folks shall see—they shall just see! (Walks about, rubbing his hands.) There will be a nice upset in the town, Katherine; you can't imagine what it will be. All the conduit-pipes will have to be relaid.

Hovstad (getting up). All the conduit-pipes—?

Dr. Stockmann. Yes, of course. The intake is too low down; it will have to be lifted to a position much higher up.

Petra. Then you were right after all.

Dr. Stockmann. Ah, you remember, Petra—I wrote opposing the plans before the work was begun. But at that time no one would listen to me. Well, I am going to let them have it now. Of course I have prepared a report for the Baths Committee; I have had it ready for a week, and was only waiting for this to come. (Shows the letter.) Now it shall go off at once. (Goes into his room and comes back with some papers.) Look at that! Four closely written sheets!—and the letter shall go with them. Give me a bit of paper, Katherine—something to wrap them up in.

That will do! Now give it to-to-(stamps his foot)—what the deuce is her name?—give it to the maid, and tell her to take it at once to the Mayor.

(Mrs. Stockmann takes the packet and goes out through the dining-room.)

Petra. What do you think Uncle Peter will say, father?

Dr. Stockmann. What is there for him to say? I should think he would be very glad that such an important truth has been brought to light.

Hovstad. Will you let me print a short note about your discovery in the "Messenger?"

Dr. Stockmann. I shall be very much obliged if you will.

Hovstad. It is very desirable that the public should be informed of it without delay.

Dr. Stockmann. Certainly.

Mrs. Stockmann (coming back). She has just gone with it.

Billing. Upon my soul, Doctor, you are going to be the foremost man in the town!

Dr. Stockmann (walking about happily). Nonsense! As a matter of

fact I have done nothing more than my duty. I have only made a lucky find—that's all. Still, all the same...

Billing. Hovstad, don't you think the town ought to give Dr. Stockmann some sort of testimonial?

Hovstad. I will suggest it, anyway.

Billing. And I will speak to Aslaksen about it.

Dr. Stockmann. No, my good friends, don't let us have any of that nonsense. I won't hear anything of the kind. And if the Baths Committee should think of voting me an increase of salary, I will not accept it. Do you hear, Katherine?—I won't accept it.

Mrs. Stockmann. You are quite right, Thomas.

Petra (lifting her glass). Your health, father!

Hovstad and Billing. Your health, Doctor! Good health!

Horster (touches glasses with DR. STOCKMANN). I hope it will bring you nothing but good luck.

Dr. Stockmann. Thank you, thank you, my dear fellows! I feel tremendously happy! It is a splendid thing for a man to be able to feel that he has done a service to his native town and to his fellow-citizens. Hurrah, Katherine! (He puts his arms round her and whirls her round and round, while she protests with laughing cries. They all laugh, clap their hands, and cheer the DOCTOR. The boys put their heads in at the door to see what is going on.)

ACT II

(SCENE.—The same. The door into the dining room is shut. It is morning. MRS. STOCKMANN, with a sealed letter in her hand, comes in from the dining room, goes to the door of the DOCTOR'S study, and peeps in.)

Mrs. Stockmann. Are you in, Thomas?

Dr. Stockmann (from within his room). Yes, I have just come in. (Comes into the room.) What is it?

Mrs. Stockmann. A letter from your brother.

Dr. Stockmann. Aha, let us see! (Opens the letter and reads:) "I return herewith the manuscript you sent me" (reads on in a low murmur) H'm!—

Mrs. Stockmann. What does he say?

Dr. Stockmann (putting the papers in his pocket). Oh, he only writes that he will come up here himself about midday.

Mrs. Stockmann. Well, try and remember to be at home this time.

Dr. Stockmann. That will be all right; I have got through all my morning visits.

Mrs. Stockmann. I am extremely curious to know how he takes it.

Dr. Stockmann. You will see he won't like it's having been I, and not he, that made the discovery.

Mrs. Stockmann. Aren't you a little nervous about that?

Dr. Stockmann. Oh, he really will be pleased enough, you know. But, at the same time, Peter is so confoundedly afraid of anyone's doing any service to the town except himself.

Mrs. Stockmann. I will tell you what, Thomas—you should be good natured, and share the credit of this with him. Couldn't you make out that it was he who set you on the scent of this discovery?

Dr. Stockmann. I am quite willing. If only I can get the thing set right. I—

(MORTEN KIIL puts his head in through the door leading from the hall, looks around in an enquiring manner, and chuckles.)

Morten Kiil (slyly). Is it—is it true?

Mrs. Stockmann (going to the door). Father!—is it you?

Dr. Stockmann. Ah, Mr. Kiil—good morning, good morning!

Mrs. Stockmann. But come along in.

Morten Kiil. If it is true, I will; if not, I am off.

Dr. Stockmann. If what is true?

Morten Kiil. This tale about the water supply, is it true?

Dr. Stockmann. Certainly it is true, but how did you come to hear it?

Morten Kiil (coming in). Petra ran in on her way to the school—

Dr. Stockmann. Did she?

Morten Kiil. Yes; and she declares that—I thought she was only making a fool of me—but it isn't like Petra to do that.

Dr. Stockmann. Of course not. How could you imagine such a thing!

Morten Kiil. Oh well, it is better never to trust anybody; you may find you have been made a fool of before you know where you are. But it is really true, all the same?

Dr. Stockmann. You can depend upon it that it is true. Won't you sit down? (Settles him on the couch.) Isn't it a real bit of luck for the town—

Morten Kiil (suppressing his laughter). A bit of luck for the town?

Dr. Stockmann. Yes, that I made the discovery in good time.

Morten Kiil (as before). Yes, yes. Yes!—But I should never have thought you the sort of man to pull your own brother's leg like this!

Dr. Stockmann. Pull his leg!

Mrs. Stockmann. Really, father dear—

Morten Kiil (resting his hands and his chin on the handle of his stick and winking slyly at the DOCTOR). Let me see, what was the story? Some kind of beast that had got into the water-pipes, wasn't it?

Dr. Stockmann. Infusoria—yes.

Morten Kiil. And a lot of these beasts had got in, according to Petra—a tremendous lot.

Dr. Stockmann. Certainly; hundreds of thousands of them, robably.

Morten Kiil. But no one can see them—isn't that so?

Dr. Stockmann. Yes; you can't see them,

Morten Kiil (with a quiet chuckle). Damn—it's the finest story I have ever heard!

Dr. Stockmann. What do you mean?

Morten Kiil. But you will never get the Mayor to believe a thing like that.

Dr. Stockmann. We shall see.

Morten Kiil. Do you think he will be fool enough to—?

Dr. Stockmann. I hope the whole town will be fools enough.

Morten Kiil. The whole town! Well, it wouldn't be a bad thing. It would just serve them right, and teach them a lesson. They think themselves so much cleverer than we old fellows. They hounded me out of the council; they did, I tell you—they hounded me out. Now they shall pay for it. You pull their legs too, Thomas!

Dr. Stockmann. Really, I—

Morten Kiil. You pull their legs! (Gets up.) If you can work it so that the Mayor and his friends all swallow the same bait, I will give ten pounds to a charity—like a shot!

Dr. Stockmann. That is very kind of you.

Morten Kiil. Yes, I haven't got much money to throw away, I can tell you; but, if you can work this, I will give five pounds to a charity at Christmas.

(HOVSTAD comes in by the hall door.)

Hovstad. Good morning! (Stops.) Oh, I beg your pardon

Dr. Stockmann. Not at all; come in.

Morten Kiil (with another chuckle). Oho!—is he in this too?

Hovstad. What do you mean?

Dr. Stockmann. Certainly he is.

Morten Kiil. I might have known it! It must get into the papers. You know how to do it, Thomas! Set your wits to work. Now I must go.

Dr. Stockmann. Won't you stay a little while?

Morten Kiil. No, I must be off now. You keep up this game for all it is worth; you won't repent it, I'm damned if you will!

(He goes out; MRS. STOCKMANN follows him into the hall.)

Dr. Stockmann (laughing). Just imagine—the old chap doesn't believe a word of all this about the water supply.

Hovstad. Oh that was it, then?

Dr. Stockmann. Yes, that was what we were talking about. Perhaps it is the same thing that brings you here?

Hovstad. Yes, it is, Can you spare me a few minutes, Doctor?

Dr. Stockmann. As long as you like, my dear fellow.

Hovstad. Have you heard from the Mayor yet?

Dr. Stockmann. Not yet. He is coming here later.

Hovstad. I have given the matter a great deal of thought since last night.

Dr. Stockmann. Well?

Hovstad. From your point of view, as a doctor and a man of science, this affair of the water supply is an isolated matter. I mean, you do not realise that it involves a great many other things.

Dr. Stockmann. How do you mean?—Let us sit down, my dear fellow. No, sit here on the couch. (HOVSTAD Sits down on the couch, DR. STOCKMANN On a chair on the other side of the table.) Now then. You mean that—?

Hovstad. You said yesterday that the pollution of the water was due to impurities in the soil.

Dr. Stockmann. Yes, unquestionably it is due to that poisonous morass up at Molledal.

Hovstad. Begging your pardon, Doctor, I fancy it is due to quite another morass altogether.

Dr. Stockmann. What morass?

Hovstad. The morass that the whole life of our town is built on and is rotting in.

Dr. Stockmann. What the deuce are you driving at, Hovstad?

Hovstad. The whole of the town's interests have, little by little, got into the hands of a pack of officials.

Dr. Stockmann. Oh, come!—they are not all officials.

Hovstad. No, but those that are not officials are at any rate the officials' friends and adherents; it is the wealthy folk, the old families in the town, that have got us entirely in their hands.

Dr. Stockmann. Yes, but after all they are men of ability and knowledge.

Hovstad. Did they show any ability or knowledge when they laid the conduit pipes where they are now?

Dr. Stockmann. No, of course that was a great piece of stupidity on their part. But that is going to be set right now.

Hovstad. Do you think that will be all such plain sailing?

Dr. Stockmann. Plain sailing or no, it has got to be done, anyway.

Hovstad. Yes, provided the press takes up the question.

Dr. Stockmann. I don't think that will be necessary, my dear fellow, I am certain my brother—

Hovstad. Excuse me, doctor; I feel bound to tell you I am inclined to take the matter up.

Dr. Stockmann. In the paper?

Hovstad. Yes. When I took over the "People's Messenger" my idea was to break up this ring of self-opinionated old fossils who had got hold of all the influence.

Dr. Stockmann. But you know you told me yourself what the result had been; you nearly ruined your paper.

Hovstad. Yes, at the time we were obliged to climb down a peg or two, it is quite true—because there was a danger of the whole project of the Baths coming to nothing if they failed us. But now the scheme has been carried through, and we can dispense with these grand gentlemen.

Dr. Stockmann. Dispense with them, yes; but, we owe them a great debt of gratitude.

Hovstad. That shall be recognised ungrudgingly, But a journalist of my democratic tendencies cannot let such an opportunity as this slip. The bubble of official infallibility must be pricked. This superstition must be destroyed, like any other.

Dr. Stockmann. I am whole-heartedly with you in that, Mr. Hovstad; if it is a superstition, away with it!

Hovstad. I should be very reluctant to bring the Mayor into it, because he is your brother. But I am sure you will agree with me that truth should be the first consideration.

Dr. Stockmann. That goes without saying. (With sudden emphasis.) Yes, but—but—

Hovstad. You must not misjudge me. I am neither more self-interested nor more ambitious than most men.

Dr. Stockmann. My dear fellow—who suggests anything of the kind?

Hovstad. I am of humble origin, as you know; and that has given me opportunities of knowing what is the most crying need in the humbler ranks of life. It is that they should be allowed some part in the direction of public affairs, Doctor. That is what will develop their faculties and intelligence and self respect—

Dr. Stockmann. I quite appreciate that.

Hovstad. Yes—and in my opinion a journalist incurs a heavy responsibility if he neglects a favourable opportunity of emancipating the masses—the humble and oppressed. I know well enough that in exalted circles I shall be called an agitator, and all that sort of thing; but they may call what they like. If only my conscience doesn't reproach me, then—

Dr. Stockmann. Quite right! Quite right, Mr. Hovstad. But all the same—devil take it! (A knock is heard at the door.) Come in!

(ASLAKSEN appears at the door. He is poorly but decently dressed, in black, with a slightly crumpled white neckcloth; he wears gloves and has a felt hat in his hand.)

Aslaksen (bowing). Excuse my taking the liberty, Doctor—

Dr. Stockmann (getting up). Ah, it is you, Aslaksen!

Aslaksen. Yes, Doctor.

Hovstad (standing up). Is it me you want, Aslaksen?

Aslaksen. No; I didn't know I should find you here. No, it was the Doctor I—

Dr. Stockmann. I am quite at your service. What is it?

Aslaksen. Is what I heard from Mr. Billing true, sir—that you mean to improve our water supply?

Dr. Stockmann. Yes, for the Baths.

Aslaksen. Quite so, I understand. Well, I have come to say that I will back that up by every means in my power.

Hovstad (to the DOCTOR). You see!

Dr. Stockmann. I shall be very grateful to you, but—

Aslaksen. Because it may be no bad thing to have us small tradesmen at your back. We form, as it were, a compact majority in the town—if we choose. And it is always a good thing to have the majority with you, Doctor.

Dr. Stockmann. That is undeniably true; but I confess I don't see why such unusual precautions should be necessary in this case. It seems to me that such a plain, straightforward thing—

Aslaksen. Oh, it may be very desirable, all the same. I know our local authorities so well; officials are not generally very ready to act on proposals that come from other people. That is why I think it would not be at all amiss if we made a little demonstration.

Hovstad. That's right.

Dr. Stockmann. Demonstration, did you say? What on earth are you going to make a demonstration about?

Aslaksen. We shall proceed with the greatest moderation, Doctor. Moderation is always my aim; it is the greatest virtue in a citizen—at least, I think so.

Dr. Stockmann. It is well known to be a characteristic of yours, Mr. Aslaksen.

Aslaksen. Yes, I think I may pride myself on that. And this matter of the water supply is of the greatest importance to us small tradesmen. The Baths promise to be a regular gold-mine for the town. We shall all make our living out of them, especially those of us who are householders. That is why we will back up the project as strongly as possible. And as I am at present Chairman of the Householders' Association.

Dr. Stockmann. Yes—?

Aslaksen. And, what is more, local secretary of the Temperance Society—you know, sir, I suppose, that I am a worker in the temperance cause?

Dr. Stockmann. Of course, of course.

Aslaksen. Well, you can understand that I come into contact with a great many people. And as I have the reputation of a temperate and law-abiding citizen—like yourself, Doctor—I have a certain influence in the town, a little bit of power, if I may be allowed to say so.

Dr. Stockmann. I know that quite well, Mr. Aslaksen.

Aslaksen. So you see it would be an easy matter for

me to set on foot some testimonial, if necessary.

Dr. Stockmann. A testimonial?

Aslaksen. Yes, some kind of an address of thanks from the townsmen for your share in a matter of such importance to the community. I need scarcely say that it would have to be drawn up with the greatest regard to moderation, so as not to offend the authorities—who, after all, have the reins in their hands. If we pay strict attention to that, no one can take it amiss, I should think!

Hovstad. Well, and even supposing they didn't like it—

Aslaksen. No, no, no; there must be no discourtesy to the authorities, Mr. Hovstad. It is no use falling foul of those upon whom our welfare so closely depends. I have done that in my time, and no good ever comes of it. But no one can take exception to a reasonable and frank expression of a citizen's views.

Dr. Stockmann (shaking him by the hand). I can't tell you, dear Mr. Aslaksen, how extremely pleased I am to find such hearty support among my fellow-citizens. I am delighted—delighted! Now, you will take a small glass of sherry, eh?

Aslaksen. No, thank you; I never drink alcohol of that kind.

Dr. Stockmann. Well, what do you say to a glass of beer, then?

Aslaksen. Nor that either, thank you, Doctor. I never drink anything as early as this. I am going into town now to talk this over with one or two householders, and prepare the ground.

Dr. Stockmann. It is tremendously kind of you, Mr. Aslaksen; but I really cannot understand the necessity for all these precautions. It seems to me that the thing should go of itself.

Aslaksen. The authorities are somewhat slow to move, Doctor. Far be it from me to seem to blame them—

Hovstad. We are going to stir them up in the paper tomorrow, Aslaksen.

Aslaksen. But not violently, I trust, Mr. Hovstad. Proceed with moderation, or you will do nothing with them. You may take my advice; I have gathered my experience in the school of life. Well, I must say goodbye, Doctor. You know now that we small tradesmen are at your back at all events, like a solid wall. You have the compact majority on your side Doctor.

Dr. Stockmann. I am very much obliged, dear Mr. Aslaksen, (Shakes hands with him.) Goodbye, goodbye.

Aslaksen. Are you going my way, towards the printing-office. Mr. Hovstad?

Hovstad, I will come later; I have something to settle up first.

Aslaksen. Very well. (Bows and goes out; STOCKMANN follows him into the hall.)

Hovstad (as STOCKMANN comes in again). Well, what do you think of that, Doctor? Don't you think it is high time we stirred a little life into all this slackness and vacillation and cowardice?

Dr. Stockmann. Are you referring to Aslaksen?

Hovstad, Yes, I am. He is one of those who are floundering in a bog—decent enough fellow though he may be, otherwise. And most of the people here are in just the same case—see-sawing and edging first to one side and then to the other, so overcome with caution and scruple that they never dare to take any decided step.

Dr. Stockmann, Yes, but Aslaksen seemed to me so thoroughly well-intentioned.

Hovstad. There is one thing I esteem higher than that; and that is for a man to be self-reliant and sure of himself.

Dr. Stockmann. I think you are perfectly right there.

Hovstad. That is why I want to seize this opportunity, and try if I cannot manage to put a little virility into these well-intentioned people for once. The idol of Authority must be shattered in this town. This gross and inexcusable blunder about the water supply must be brought home to the mind of every municipal voter.

Dr. Stockmann. Very well; if you are of opinion that it is for the good of the community, so be it. But not until I have had a talk with my brother.

Hovstad. Anyway, I will get a leading article ready; and if the Mayor refuses to take the matter up—

Dr. Stockmann. How can you suppose such a thing possible!

Hovstad. It is conceivable. And in that case—

Dr. Stockmann. In that case I promise you—. Look here, in that case you may print my report—every word of it.

Hovstad. May I? Have I your word for it?

Dr. Stockmann (giving him the MS.). Here it is; take it with you. It can do no harm for you to read it through, and you can give it me back later on.

Hovstad. Good, good! That is what I will do. And now goodbye, Doctor.

Dr. Stockmann. Goodbye, goodbye. You will see everything will run quite smoothly, Mr. Hovstad—quite smoothly.

Hovstad. Hm!—we shall see. (Bows and goes out.)

Dr. Stockmann (opens the dining-room door and looks in). Katherine! Oh, you are back, Petra?

Petra (coming in). Yes, I have just come from the school.

Mrs. Stockmann (coming in). Has he not been here yet?

Dr. Stockmann. Peter? No, but I have had a long talk with Hovstad. He is quite excited about my discovery, I find it has a much wider bearing than I at first imagined. And he has put his paper at my disposal if necessity should arise.

Mrs. Stockmann. Do you think it will?

Dr. Stockmann. Not for a moment. But at all events it makes me feel proud to know that I have the liberal-minded independent press on my side. Yes, and just imagine—I have had a visit from the Chairman of the Householders' Association!

Mrs. Stockmann. Oh! What did he want?

Dr. Stockmann. To offer me his support too. They will support me in a body if it should be necessary. Katherine—do you know what I have got behind me?

Mrs. Stockmann. Behind you? No, what have you got behind you?

Dr. Stockmann. The compact majority.

Mrs. Stockmann. Really? Is that a good thing for you Thomas?

Dr. Stockmann. I should think it was a good thing. (Walks up and down rubbing his hands.) By Jove, it's a fine thing to feel this bond of brotherhood between oneself and one's fellow citizens!

Petra. And to be able to do so much that is good and useful, father!

Dr. Stockmann. And for one's own native town into the bargain, my child!

Mrs. Stockmann. That was a ring at the bell.

Dr. Stockmann. It must be he, then. (A knock is heard at the door.) Come in!

Peter Stockmann (comes in from the hall). Good morning.

Dr. Stockmann. Glad to see you, Peter!

Mrs. Stockmann. Good morning, Peter, How are you?

Peter Stockmann. So so, thank you. (To Dr. Stockmann.) I received from you yesterday, after office hours, a report dealing with the condition of the water at the Baths.

Dr. Stockmann. Yes. Have you read it?

Peter Stockmann. Yes, I have,

Dr. Stockmann. And what have you to say to it?

Peter Stockmann (with a sidelong glance). Hm!—

Mrs. Stockmann. Come along, Petra. (She and PETRA go into the room on the left.)

Peter Stockmann (after a pause). Was it necessary to make all these investigations behind my back?

Dr. Stockmann. Yes, because until I was absolutely certain about it—

Peter Stockmann. Then you mean that you are absolutely certain now?

Dr. Stockmann. Surely you are convinced of that.

Peter Stockmann. Is it your intention to bring this document before the Baths Committee as a sort of official communication?

Dr. Stockmann. Certainly. Something must be done in the matter—and that quickly.

Peter Stockmann. As usual, you employ violent expressions in your report. You say, amongst other things, that what we offer visitors in our Baths is a permanent supply of poison.

Dr. Stockmann. Well, can you describe it any other way,

Peter? Just think—water that is poisonous, whether you drink it or bathe in it! And this we offer to the poor sick folk who come to us trustfully and pay us at an exorbitant rate to be made well again!

Peter Stockmann. And your reasoning leads you to this conclusion, that we must build a sewer to draw off the alleged impurities from Molledal and must relay the water conduits.

Dr. Stockmann. Yes. Do you see any other way out of it? I don't.

Peter Stockmann. I made a pretext this morning to go and see the town engineer, and, as if only half seriously, broached the subject of these proposals as a thing we might perhaps have to take under consideration some time later on.

Dr. Stockmann. Some time later on!

Peter Stockmann. He smiled at what he considered to be my extravagance, naturally. Have you taken the trouble to consider what your proposed alterations would cost? According to the information I obtained, the expenses would probably mount up to fifteen or twenty thousand pounds.

Dr. Stockmann. Would it cost so much?

Peter Stockmann. Yes; and the worst part of it would be that the work would take at least two years.

Dr. Stockmann. Two years? Two whole years?

Peter Stockmann. At least. And what are we to do with the Baths in the meantime? Close them? Indeed we should be obliged to. And do you suppose anyone would come near the place after it had got out that the water was dangerous?

Dr. Stockmann. Yes but, Peter, that is what it is.

Peter Stockmann. And all this at this juncture—just as the

Baths are beginning to be known. There are other towns in the neighbourhood with qualifications to attract visitors for bathing purposes. Don't you suppose they would immediately strain every nerve to divert the entire stream of strangers to themselves? Unquestionably they would; and then where should we be? We should probably have to abandon the whole thing, which has cost us so much money-and then you would have ruined your native town.

Dr. Stockmann. I—should have ruined—!

Peter Stockmann. It is simply and solely through the Baths that the town has before it any future worth mentioning. You know that just as well as I.

Dr. Stockmann. But what do you think ought to be done, then?

Peter Stockmann. Your report has not convinced me that the condition of the water at the Baths is as bad as you represent it to be.

Dr. Stockmann. I tell you it is even worse!—or at all events it will be in summer, when the warm weather comes.

Peter Stockmann. As I said, I believe you exaggerate the matter considerably. A capable physician ought to know what measures to take—he ought to be capable of preventing injurious influences or of remedying them if they become obviously persistent.

Dr. Stockmann. Well? What more?

Peter Stockmann. The water supply for the Baths is now an established fact, and in consequence must be treated as such. But probably the Committee, at its discretion, will not be disinclined to consider the question of how far it might be possible to introduce certain improvements consistently with a reasonable expenditure.

Dr. Stockmann. And do you suppose that I will have anything to do with such a piece of trickery as that?

Peter Stockmann. Trickery!!

Dr. Stockmann. Yes, it would be a trick—a fraud, a lie, a downright crime towards the public, towards the whole community!

Peter Stockmann. I have not, as I remarked before, been able to convince myself that there is actually any imminent danger.

Dr. Stockmann. You have! It is impossible that you should not be convinced. I know I have represented the facts absolutely truthfully and fairly. And you know it very well, Peter, only you won't acknowledge it. It was owing to your action that both the Baths and the water conduits were built where they are; and that is what you won't acknowledge—that damnable blunder of yours. Pooh!—do you suppose I don't see through you?

Peter Stockmann. And even if that were true? If I perhaps guard my reputation somewhat anxiously, it is in the interests of the town. Without moral authority I am powerless to direct public affairs as seems, to my judgment, to be best for the common good. And on that account—and for various other reasons too—it appears to me to be a matter of importance that your report should not be delivered to the Committee. In the interests of the public, you must withhold it. Then, later on, I will raise the question and we will do our best, privately; but nothing of this unfortunate affair not a single word of it—must come to the ears of the public.

Dr. Stockmann. I am afraid you will not be able to prevent that now, my dear Peter.

Peter Stockmann. It must and shall be prevented.

Dr. Stockmann. It is no use, I tell you. There are too many people that know about it.

Peter Stockmann. That know about it? Who? Surely you don't mean those fellows on the "People's Messenger"?

Dr. Stockmann. Yes, they know. The liberal-minded independent press is going to see that you do your duty.

Peter Stockmann (after a short pause). You are an extraordinarily independent man, Thomas. Have you given no thought to the consequences this may have for yourself?

Dr. Stockmann. Consequences?—for me?

Peter Stockmann. For you and yours, yes.

Dr. Stockmann. What the deuce do you mean?

Peter Stockmann. I believe I have always behaved in a brotherly way to you—haven't I always been ready to oblige or to help you?

Dr. Stockmann. Yes, you have, and I am grateful to you for it.

Peter Stockmann. There is no need. Indeed, to some extent I was forced to do so—for my own sake. I always hoped that, if I helped to improve your financial position, I should be able to keep some check on you.

Dr. Stockmann. What! Then it was only for your own sake—!

Peter Stockmann. Up to a certain point, yes. It is painful for a man in an official position to have his nearest relative compromising himself time after time.

Dr. Stockmann. And do you consider that I do that?

Peter Stockmann. Yes, unfortunately, you do, without even being aware of it. You have a restless, pugnacious, rebellious disposition. And then there is that disastrous propensity of yours to want to write about every sort of possible and impossible thing. The moment an idea comes into your head, you must needs go and write a newspaper article or a whole pamphlet about it.

Dr. Stockmann. Well, but is it not the duty of a citizen to let the public share in any new ideas he may have?

Peter Stockmann. Oh, the public doesn't require any new ideas. The public is best served by the good, old established ideas it already has.

Dr. Stockmann. And that is your honest opinion?

Peter Stockmann. Yes, and for once I must talk frankly to you. Hitherto I have tried to avoid doing so, because I know how irritable you are; but now I must tell you the truth, Thomas. You have no conception what an amount of harm you do yourself by your impetuosity. You complain of the authorities, you even complain of the government—you are always pulling them to pieces; you insist that you have been neglected and persecuted. But what else can such a cantankerous man as you expect?

Dr. Stockmann. What next! Cantankerous, am I?

Peter Stockmann. Yes, Thomas, you are an extremely cantankerous man to work with—I know that to my cost. You disregard everything that you ought to have consideration for. You seem completely to forget that it is me you have to thank for your appointment here as medical officer to the Baths.

Dr. Stockmann. I was entitled to it as a matter of course!—I and nobody else! I was the first person to see that the town could be made into a flourishing watering-place, and I was the only one who saw it at that time. I had to fight single-handed in support of the idea for many years; and I wrote and wrote—

Peter Stockmann. Undoubtedly. But things were not ripe for the scheme then—though, of course, you could not judge of that in your out-of-the-way corner up north. But as soon as the opportune moment came I—and the others—took the matter into our hands.

Dr. Stockmann. Yes, and made this mess of all my beautiful plan. It is pretty obvious now what clever fellows you were!

Peter Stockmann. To my mind the whole thing only seems to mean that you are seeking another outlet for your combativeness. You want to pick a quarrel with your superiors—an old habit of yours. You cannot put up with any authority over you. You look askance at anyone who occupies a superior official position; you regard him as a personal enemy, and then any stick is good enough to beat him with. But now I have called your attention to the fact that the town's interests are at stake—and, incidentally, my own too. And therefore, I must tell you, Thomas, that you will find me inexorable with regard to what I am about to require you to do.

Dr. Stockmann. And what is that?

Peter Stockmann. As you have been so indiscreet as to speak of this delicate matter to outsiders, despite the fact that you ought to have treated it as entirely official and confidential, it is obviously impossible to hush it up now. All sorts of rumours will get about directly, and everybody who has a grudge against us will take care to embellish these rumours. So it will be necessary for you to refute them publicly.

Dr. Stockmann. I! How? I don't understand.

Peter Stockmann. What we shall expect is that, after making further investigations, you will come to the conclusion that the matter is not by any means as dangerous or as critical as you imagined in the first instance.

Dr. Stockmann. Oho!—so that is what you expect!

Peter Stockmann. And, what is more, we shall expect you to make public profession of your confidence in the Committee and in their readiness to consider fully and conscientiously what steps may be necessary to remedy any possible defects.

Dr. Stockmann. But you will never be able to do that by patching and tinkering at it—never! Take my word for it, Peter; I mean what I say, as deliberately and emphatically as possible.

Peter Stockmann. As an officer under the Committee, you have no right to any individual opinion.

Dr. Stockmann (amazed). No right?

Peter Stockmann. In your official capacity, no. As a private person, it is quite another matter. But as a subordinate member of the staff of the Baths, you have no right to express any opinion which runs contrary to that of your superiors.

Dr. Stockmann. This is too much! I, a doctor, a man of science, have no right to—!

Peter Stockmann. The matter in hand is not simply a scientific one. It is a complicated matter, and has its economic as well as its technical side.

Dr. Stockmann. I don't care what it is! I intend to be free to express my opinion on any subject under the sun.

Peter Stockmann. As you please—but not on any subject concerning the Baths. That we forbid.

Dr. Stockmann (shouting). You forbid—! You! A pack of—

Peter Stockmann. I forbid it—I, your chief; and if I forbid it, you have to obey.

Dr. Stockmann (controlling himself). Peter—if you were not my brother—

Petra (throwing open the door). Father, you shan't stand this!

Mrs. Stockmann (coming in after her). Petra, Petra!

Peter Stockmann. Oh, so you have been eavesdropping.

Mrs. Stockmann. You were talking so loud, we couldn't help it!

Petra. Yes, I was listening.

Peter Stockmann. Well, after all, I am very glad—

Dr. Stockmann (going up to him). You were saying something about forbidding and obeying?

Peter Stockmann. You obliged me to take that tone with you.

Dr. Stockmann. And so I am to give myself the lie, publicly?

Peter Stockmann. We consider it absolutely necessary that you should make some such public statement as I have asked for.

Dr. Stockmann. And if I do not—obey?

Peter Stockmann. Then we shall publish a statement ourselves to reassure the public.

Dr. Stockmann. Very well; but in that case I shall use my pen against you. I stick to what I have said; I will show that I am right and that you are wrong. And what will you do then?

Peter Stockmann. Then I shall not be able to prevent your being dismissed.

Dr. Stockmann. What—?

Petra. Father—dismissed!

Mrs. Stockmann. Dismissed!

Peter Stockmann. Dismissed from the staff of the Baths. I shall be obliged to propose that you shall immediately be given notice, and shall not be allowed any further participation in the Baths' affairs.

Dr. Stockmann. You would dare to do that!

Peter Stockmann. It is you that are playing the daring game.

Petra. Uncle, that is a shameful way to treat a man like father!

Mrs. Stockmann. Do hold your tongue, Petra!

Peter Stockmann (looking at PETRA). Oh, so we volunteer our opinions already, do we? Of course. (To MRS. STOCKMANN.) Katherine, I imagine you are the most sensible person in this house. Use any influence you may have over your husband, and make him see what this will entail for his family as well as—

Dr. Stockmann. My family is my own concern and nobody else's!

Peter Stockmann. —for his own family, as I was saying, as well as for the town he lives in.

Dr. Stockmann. It is I who have the real good of the town at heart! I want to lay bare the defects that sooner or later must come to the light of day. I will show whether I love my native town.

Peter Stockmann. You, who in your blind obstinacy want to cut off the most important source of the town's welfare?

Dr. Stockmann. The source is poisoned, man! Are you mad? We are making our living by retailing filth and corruption! The whole of our flourishing municipal life derives its sustenance from a lie!

Peter Stockmann. All imagination—or something even worse. The man who can throw out such offensive insinuations about his native town must be an enemy to our community.

Dr. Stockmann (going up to him). Do you dare to—!

Mrs. Stockmann (throwing herself between them). Thomas!

Petra (catching her father by the arm). Don't lose

your temper, father!

Peter Stockmann. I will not expose myself to violence. Now you have had a warning; so reflect on what you owe to yourself and your family. Good-bye. (Goes out.)

Dr. Stockmann (walking up and down). Am I to put up with such treatment as this? In my own house, Katherine! What do you think of that!

Mrs. Stockmann. Indeed it is both shameful and absurd, Thomas—

Petra. If only I could give uncle a piece of my mind—

Dr. Stockmann. It is my own fault. I ought to have flown out at him long ago!—shown my teeth!—bitten! To hear him call me an enemy to our community! Me! I shall not take that lying down, upon my soul!

Mrs. Stockmann. But, dear Thomas, your brother has power on his side.

Dr. Stockmann. Yes, but I have right on mine, I tell you.

Mrs. Stockmann. Oh yes, right—right. What is the use of having right on your side if you have not got might?

Petra. Oh, mother!—how can you say such a thing!

Dr. Stockmann. Do you imagine that in a free country it is no use having right on your side? You are absurd, Katherine. Besides, haven't I got the liberal-minded, independent press to lead the way, and the compact majority behind me? That is might enough, I should think!

Mrs. Stockmann. But, good heavens, Thomas, you don't mean to?

Dr. Stockmann. Don't mean to what?

Mrs. Stockmann. To set yourself up in opposition to your brother.

Dr. Stockmann. In God's name, what else do you suppose I should do but take my stand on right and truth?

Petra. Yes, I was just going to say that.

Mrs. Stockmann. But it won't do you any earthly good. If they won't do it, they won't.

Dr. Stockmann. Oho, Katherine! Just give me time, and you will see how I will carry the war into their camp.

Mrs. Stockmann. Yes, you carry the war into their camp, and you get your dismissal—that is what you will do.

Dr. Stockmann. In any case I shall have done my duty towards the public—towards the community, I, who am called its enemy!

Mrs. Stockmann. But towards your family, Thomas? Towards your own home! Do you think that is doing your duty towards those you have to provide for?

Petra. Ah, don't think always first of us, mother.

Mrs. Stockmann. Oh, it is easy for you to talk; you are able to shift for yourself, if need be. But remember the boys, Thomas; and think a little of yourself too, and of me—

Dr. Stockmann. I think you are out of your senses, Katherine! If I were to be such a miserable coward as to go on my knees to Peter and his damned crew, do you suppose I should ever know an hour's peace of mind all my life afterwards?

Mrs. Stockmann. I don't know anything about that; but God preserve us from the peace of mind we shall have, all the same, if you go on defying him! You will find yourself again without the means of subsistence, with no income to count upon. I should think we had had enough of that in the old days. Remember that, Thomas; think what that means.

Dr. Stockmann (collecting himself with a struggle and clenching his fists). And this is what this slavery can bring upon a free, honourable man! Isn't it horrible, Katherine?

Mrs. Stockmann. Yes, it is sinful to treat you so, it is perfectly true. But, good heavens, one has to put up with so much injustice in this world. There are the boys, Thomas! Look at them! What is to become of them? Oh, no, no, you can never have the heart—. (EJLIF and MORTEN have come in, while she was speaking, with their school books in their hands.)

Dr. Stockmann. The boys— I (Recovers himself suddenly.) No, even if the whole world goes to pieces, I will never bow my neck to this yokel (Goes towards his room.)

Mrs. Stockmann (following him). Thomas—what are you going to do!

Dr. Stockmann (at his door). I mean to have the right to look my sons in the face when they are grown men. (Goes into his room.)

Mrs. Stockmann (bursting into tears). God help us all!

Petra. Father is splendid! He will not give in.

(The boys look on in amazement; PETRA signs to them not to speak.)

ACT III

(SCENE.—The editorial office of the "People's Messenger." The entrance door is on the left-hand side of the back wall; on the right-hand side is another door with glass panels through which the printing room can be seen. Another door in the right-hand wall. In the middle of the room is a large table covered with papers, newspapers and books. In the foreground on the left a window, before which stands a desk and a high stool. There are a couple of easy chairs by the table, and other chairs standing along the wall. The room is dingy and uncomfortable; the furniture is old, the chairs stained and torn. In the printing room the compositors are seen at work, and a printer is working a handpress. HOVSTAD is sitting at the desk, writing. BILLING comes in from the right with DR. STOCKMANN'S manuscript in his hand.)

Billing.	Well, I must say!
Hovstad	(still writing). Have you read it through?
Billing	(laying the MS. on the desk). Yes, indeed I have.
Hovstad.	Don't you think the Doctor hits them pretty hard?
Billing.	Hard? Bless my soul, he's crushing! Every word falls like—how shall I put it?—like the blow of a sledgehammer.

Hovstad. Yes, but they are not the people to throw up the sponge at the first blow.

Billing. That is true; and for that reason we must strike blow upon blow until the whole of this aristocracy tumbles to pieces. As I sat in there reading this, I almost seemed to see a revolution in being.

Hovstad (turning round). Hush!—Speak so that Aslaksen cannot hear you.

Billing lowering his voice). Aslaksen is a chicken-hearted chap, a coward; there is nothing of the man in him. But this time you will insist on your own way, won't you? You will put the Doctor's article in?

Hovstad. Yes, and if the Mayor doesn't like it—

Billing. That will be the devil of a nuisance.

Hovstad. Well, fortunately we can turn the situation to good account, whatever happens. If the Mayor will not fall in with the Doctor's project, he will have all the small tradesmen down on him—the whole of the Householders' Association and the rest of them. And if he does fall in with it, he will fall out with the whole crowd of large shareholders in the Baths, who up to now have been his most valuable supporters—

Billing. Yes, because they will certainly have to fork out a pretty penny—

Hovstad. Yes, you may be sure they will. And in this way the ring will be broken up, you see, and then in every issue of the paper we will enlighten the public on the Mayor's incapability on one point and another, and make it clear that all the positions of trust in the town, the whole control of municipal affairs, ought to be put in the hands of the Liberals.

Billing. That is perfectly true! I see it coming—I

see it coming; we are on the threshold of a revolution!

(A knock is heard at the door.)

Hovstad. Hush! (Calls out.) Come in! (DR. STOCKMANN comes in by the street door. HOVSTAD goes to meet him.) Ah, it is you, Doctor! Well?

Dr. Stockmann. You may set to work and print it, Mr. Hovstad!

Hovstad. Has it come to that, then?

Billing. Hurrah!

Dr. Stockmann. Yes, print away. Undoubtedly it has come to that. Now they must take what they get. There is going to be a fight in the town, Mr. Billing!

Billing. War to the knife, I hope! We will get our knives to their throats, Doctor!

Dr. Stockmann. This article is only a beginning. I have already got four or five more sketched out in my head. Where is Aslaksen?

Billing (calls into the printing-room). Aslaksen, just come here for a minute!

Hovstad. Four or five more articles, did you say? On the same subject?

Dr. Stockmann. No—far from it, my dear fellow. No, they are about quite another matter. But they all spring from the question of the water supply and the drainage. One thing leads to another, you know. It is like beginning to pull down an old house, exactly.

Billing. Upon my soul, it's true; you find you are not done till you have pulled all the old rubbish down.

Aslaksen (coming in). Pulled down? You are not thinking of pulling down the Baths surely, Doctor?

Hovstad. Far from it, don't be afraid.

Dr. Stockmann.	No, we meant something quite different. Well, what do you think of my article, Mr. Hovstad?
Hovstad.	I think it is simply a masterpiece.
Dr. Stockmann.	Do you really think so? Well, I am very pleased, very pleased.
Hovstad.	It is so clear and intelligible. One need have no special knowledge to understand the bearing of it. You will have every enlightened man on your side.
Aslaksen.	And every prudent man too, I hope?
Billing.	The prudent and the imprudent—almost the whole town.
Aslaksen.	In that case we may venture to print it.
Dr. Stockmann.	I should think so!
Hovstad.	We will put it in tomorrow morning.
Dr. Stockmann.	Of course—you must not lose a single day. What I wanted to ask you, Mr. Aslaksen, was if you would supervise the printing of it yourself.
Aslaksen.	With pleasure.
Dr. Stockmann.	Take care of it as if it were a treasure! No misprints—every word is important. I will look in again a little later; perhaps you will be able to let me see a proof. I can't tell you how eager I am to see it in print, and see it burst upon the public—
Billing.	Burst upon them—yes, like a flash of lightning!
Dr. Stockmann.	—and to have it submitted to the judgment of my intelligent fellow townsmen. You cannot imagine what I have gone through today. I have been threatened first with one thing and then with another; they have tried to rob me of my most elementary rights as a man—
Billing.	What! Your rights as a man!

Dr. Stockmann.	—they have tried to degrade me, to make a coward of me, to force me to put personal interests before my most sacred convictions.
Billing.	That is too much—I'm damned if it isn't.
Hovstad.	Oh, you mustn't be surprised at anything from that quarter.
Dr. Stockmann.	Well, they will get the worst of it with me; they may assure themselves of that. I shall consider the "People's Messenger" my sheet-anchor now, and every single day I will bombard them with one article after another, like bombshells—
Aslaksen.	Yes, but
Billing.	Hurrah!—it is war, it is war!
Dr. Stockmann.	I shall smite them to the ground—I shall crush them—I shall break down all their defenses, before the eyes of the honest public! That is what I shall do!
Aslaksen,	Yes, but in moderation, Doctor—proceed with moderation.
Billing.	Not a bit of it, not a bit of it! Don't spare the dynamite!
Dr. Stockmann.	Because it is not merely a question of water-supply and drains now, you know. No—it is the whole of our social life that we have got to purify and disinfect—
Billing.	Spoken like a deliverer!
Dr. Stockmann.	All the incapables must be turned out, you understand—and that in every walk of life! Endless vistas have opened themselves to my mind's eye today. I cannot see it all quite clearly yet, but I shall in time. Young and vigorous standard-bearers—those are what we need and must seek, my friends; we must have new men in command at all our outposts.

Billing. Hear hear!

Dr. Stockmann. We only need to stand by one another, and it will all be perfectly easy. The revolution will be launched like a ship that runs smoothly off the stocks. Don't you think so?

Hovstad. For my part I think we have now a prospect of getting the municipal authority into the hands where it should lie.

Aslaksen. And if only we proceed with moderation, I cannot imagine that there will be any risk.

Dr. Stockmann. Who the devil cares whether there is any risk or not! What I am doing, I am doing in the name of truth and for the sake of my conscience.

Hovstad. You are a man who deserves to be supported, Doctor.

Aslaksen. Yes, there is no denying that the Doctor is a true friend to the town—a real friend to the community, that he is.

Billing. Take my word for it, Aslaksen, Dr. Stockmann is a friend of the people.

Aslaksen. I fancy the Householders' Association will make use of that expression before long.

Dr. Stockmann (affected, grasps their hands). Thank you, thank you, my dear staunch friends. It is very refreshing to me to hear you say that; my brother called me something quite different. By Jove, he shall have it back, with interest! But now I must be off to see a poor devil—I will come back, as I said. Keep a very careful eye on the manuscript, Aslaksen, and don't for worlds leave out any of my notes of exclamation! Rather put one or two more in! Capital, capital! Well, goodbye for the present—goodbye, goodbye! (They show him to the door, and bow him out.)

Hovstad. He may prove an invaluably useful man to us.

Aslaksen. Yes, so long as he confines himself to this matter of the Baths. But if he goes farther afield, I don't think it would be advisable to follow him.

Hovstad. Hm!—that all depends—

Billing. You are so infernally timid, Aslaksen!

Aslaksen. Timid? Yes, when it is a question of the local authorities, I am timid, Mr. Billing; it is a lesson I have learned in the school of experience, let me tell you. But try me in higher politics, in matters that concern the government itself, and then see if I am timid.

Billing. No, you aren't, I admit. But this is simply contradicting yourself.

Aslaksen. I am a man with a conscience, and that is the whole matter. If you attack the government, you don't do the community any harm, anyway; those fellows pay no attention to attacks, you see—they go on just as they are, in spite of them. But local authorities are different; they can be turned out, and then perhaps you may get an ignorant lot into office who may do irreparable harm to the householders and everybody else.

Hovstad. But what of the education of citizens by self government—don't you attach any importance to that?

Aslaksen. When a man has interests of his own to protect, he cannot think of everything, Mr. Hovstad.

Hovstad. Then I hope I shall never have interests of my own to protect!

Billing. Hear, hear!

Aslaksen (with a smile). Hm! (Points to the desk.)

Mr. Sheriff Stensgaard was your predecessor at that editorial desk.

Billing (spitting). Bah! That turncoat.

Hovstad. I am not a weathercock—and never will be.

Aslaksen. A politician should never be too certain of anything, Mr. Hovstad. And as for you, Mr. Billing, I should think it is time for you to be taking in a reef or two in your sails, seeing that you are applying for the post of secretary to the Bench.

Billing. I—!

Hovstad. Are you, Billing?

Billing. Well, yes—but you must clearly understand I am only doing it to annoy the bigwigs.

Aslaksen. Anyhow, it is no business of mine. But if I am to be accused of timidity and of inconsistency in my principles, this is what I want to point out: my political past is an open book. I have never changed, except perhaps to become a little more moderate, you see. My heart is still with the people; but I don't deny that my reason has a certain bias towards the authorities—the local ones, I mean. (Goes into the printing room.)

Billing. Oughtn't we to try and get rid of him, Hovstad?

Hovstad. Do you know anyone else who will advance the money for our paper and printing bill?

Billing. It is an infernal nuisance that we don't possess some capital to trade on.

Hovstad (sitting down at his desk). Yes, if we only had that, then—

Billing. Suppose you were to apply to Dr. Stockmann?

Hovstad (turning over some papers). What is the use? He has got nothing.

Billing. No, but he has got a warm man in the background, old Morten Kiil—"the Badger," as they call him.

Hovstad (writing). Are you so sure he has got anything?

Billing. Good Lord, of course he has! And some of it must come to the Stockmanns. Most probably he will do something for the children, at all events.

Hovstad (turning half round). Are you counting on that?

Billing. Counting on it? Of course I am not counting on anything.

Hovstad. That is right. And I should not count on the secretaryship to the Bench either, if I were you; for I can assure you—you won't get it.

Billing. Do you think I am not quite aware of that? My object is precisely not to get it. A slight of that kind stimulates a man's fighting power—it is like getting a supply of fresh bile—and I am sure one needs that badly enough in a hole-and-corner place like this, where it is so seldom anything happens to stir one up.

Hovstad (writing). Quite so, quite so.

Billing. Ah, I shall be heard of yet!—Now I shall go and write the appeal to the Householders' Association. (Goes into the room on the right.)

Hovstad (sitting al his desk, biting his penholder, says slowly). Hm!—that's it, is it. (A knock is heard.) Come in! (PETRA comes in by the outer door. HOVSTAD gets up.) What, you!—here?

Petra. Yes, you must forgive me—

Hovstad (pulling a chair forward). Won't you sit down?

Petra. No, thank you; I must go again in a moment.

Hovstad. Have you come with a message from your father, by any chance?

Petra. No, I have come on my own account. (Takes a book out of her coat pocket.) Here is the English story.

Hovstad. Why have you brought it back?

Petra. Because I am not going to translate it.

Hovstad. But you promised me faithfully.

Petra. Yes, but then I had not read it, I don't suppose you have read it either?

Hovstad. No, you know quite well I don't understand English; but—

Petra. Quite so. That is why I wanted to tell you that you must find something else. (Lays the book on the table.) You can't use this for the "People's Messenger."

Hovstad. Why not?

Petra. Because it conflicts with all your opinions.

Hovstad. Oh, for that matter—

Petra. You don't understand me. The burden of this story is that there is a supernatural power that looks after the so-called good people in this world and makes everything happen for the best in their case—while all the so-called bad people are punished.

Hovstad. Well, but that is all right. That is just what our readers want.

Petra. And are you going to be the one to give it to them? For myself, I do not believe a word of it. You know quite well that things do not happen so in reality.

Hovstad. You are perfectly right; but an editor cannot always act as he would prefer. He is often obliged to bow to the wishes of the public in unimportant matters. Politics are the most important thing in life—for a newspaper, anyway; and if I want to carry my public with me on the path that leads to liberty and progress, I must not frighten them away. If they find a moral tale of this sort in the serial at the bottom of the page, they will be all the more ready to read what is printed above it; they feel more secure, as it were.

Petra. For shame! You would never go and set a snare like that for your readers; you are not a spider!

Hovstad (smiling). Thank you for having such a good opinion of me. No; as a matter of fact that is Billing's idea and not mine.

Petra. Billing's!

Hovstad. Yes; anyway, he propounded that theory here one day. And it is Billing who is so anxious to have that story in the paper; I don't know anything about the book.

Petra. But how can Billing, with his emancipated views—

Hovstad. Oh, Billing is a many-sided man. He is applying for the post of secretary to the Bench, too, I hear.

Petra. I don't believe it, Mr. Hovstad. How could he possibly bring himself to do such a thing?

Hovstad. Ah, you must ask him that.

Petra. I should never have thought it of him.

Hovstad (looking more closely at her). No? Does it really surprise you so much?

Petra. Yes. Or perhaps not altogether. Really, I don't quite know

Hovstad. We journalists are not much worth, Miss Stockmann.

Petra. Do you really mean that?

Hovstad. I think so sometimes.

Petra. Yes, in the ordinary affairs of everyday life, perhaps; I can understand that. But now, when you have taken a weighty matter in hand—

Hovstad. This matter of your father's, you mean?

Petra. Exactly. It seems to me that now you must feel you are a man worth more than most.

Hovstad. Yes, today I do feel something of that sort.

Petra. Of course you do, don't you? It is a splendid vocation you have chosen—to smooth the way for the march of unappreciated truths, and new and courageous lines of thought. If it were nothing more than because you stand fearlessly in the open and take up the cause of an injured man—

Hovstad. Especially when that injured man is—ahem!—I don't rightly know how to—

Petra. When that man is so upright and so honest, you mean?

Hovstad (more gently). Especially when he is your father I meant.

Petra (suddenly checked). That?

Hovstad. Yes, Petra—Miss Petra.

Petra. Is it that, that is first and foremost with you? Not the matter itself? Not the truth?—not my father's big generous heart?

Hovstad. Certainly—of course—that too.

Petra. No, thank you; you have betrayed yourself, Mr. Hovstad, and now I shall never trust you again in anything.

Hovstad. Can you really take it so amiss in me that it is mostly for your sake—?

Petra. What I am angry with you for, is for not having been honest with my father. You talked to him as if the truth and the good of the community were what lay nearest to your heart. You have made fools of both my father and me. You are not the man you made yourself out to be. And that I shall never forgive you-never!

Hovstad. You ought not to speak so bitterly, Miss Petra—least of all now.

Petra. Why not now, especially?

Hovstad. Because your father cannot do without my help.

Petra (looking him up and down). Are you that sort of man too? For shame!

Hovstad. No, no, I am not. This came upon me so unexpectedly—you must believe that.

Petra. I know what to believe. Goodbye.

Aslaksen (coming from the printing room, hurriedly and with an air of mystery). Damnation, Hovstad!—(Sees Petra.) Oh, this is awkward—

Petra. There is the book; you must give it to some one else. (Goes towards the door.)

Hovstad (following her). But, Miss Stockmann—

Petra. Goodbye. (Goes out.)

Aslaksen. I say—Mr. Hovstad—

Hovstad. Well well!—what is it?

Aslaksen. The Mayor is outside in the printing room.

Hovstad. The Mayor, did you say?

Aslaksen. Yes he wants to speak to you. He came in by the back door—didn't want to be seen, you understand.

Hovstad. What can he want? Wait a bit—I will go myself. (Goes to the door of the printing room, opens it, bows and invites PETER STOCKMANN in.) Just see, Aslaksen, that no one—

Aslaksen. Quite so. (Goes into the printing-room.)

Peter Stockmann. You did not expect to see me here, Mr. Hovstad?

Hovstad. No, I confess I did not.

Peter Stockmann (looking round). You are very snug in here—very nice indeed.

Hovstad. Oh—

Peter Stockmann. And here I come, without any notice, to take up your time!

Hovstad. By all means, Mr. Mayor. I am at your service. But let me relieve you of your—(takes STOCKMANN's hat and stick and puts them on a chair). Won't you sit down?

Peter Stockmann (sitting down by the table). Thank you. (HOVSTAD sits down.) I have had an extremely annoying experience to-day, Mr. Hovstad.

Hovstad. Really? Ah well, I expect with all the various business you have to attend to—

Peter Stockmann. The Medical Officer of the Baths is responsible for what happened today.

Hovstad. Indeed? The Doctor?

Peter Stockmann. He has addressed a kind of report to the Baths Committee on the subject of certain supposed defects in the Baths.

Hovstad. Has he indeed?

Peter Stockmann. Yes—has he not told you? I thought he said—

Hovstad. Ah, yes—it is true he did mention something about—

Aslaksen (coming from the printing-room). I ought to have that copy.

Hovstad (angrily). Ahem!—there it is on the desk.

Aslaksen (taking it). Right.

Peter Stockmann. But look there—that is the thing I was speaking of!

Aslaksen. Yes, that is the Doctor's article, Mr. Mayor.

Hovstad. Oh, is THAT what you were speaking about?

Peter Stockmann. Yes, that is it. What do you think of it?

Hovstad. Oh, I am only a layman—and I have only taken a very cursory glance at it.

Peter Stockmann. But you are going to print it?

Hovstad. I cannot very well refuse a distinguished man.

Aslaksen. I have nothing to do with editing the paper, Mr. Mayor—

Peter Stockmann. I understand.

Aslaksen. I merely print what is put into my hands.

Peter Stockmann. Quite so.

Aslaksen. And so I must— (moves off towards the printing-room).

Peter Stockmann. No, but wait a moment, Mr. Aslaksen. You will allow me, Mr. Hovstad?

Hovstad. If you please, Mr. Mayor.

Peter Stockmann. You are a discreet and thoughtful man, Mr. Aslaksen.

Aslaksen. I am delighted to hear you think so, sir.

Peter Stockmann. And a man of very considerable influence.

Aslaksen. Chiefly among the small tradesmen, sir.

Peter Stockmann. The small tax-payers are the majority—here as everywhere else.

Aslaksen. That is true.

Peter Stockmann. And I have no doubt you know the general trend of opinion among them, don't you?

Aslaksen. Yes I think I may say I do, Mr. Mayor.

Peter Stockmann. Yes. Well, since there is such a praiseworthy spirit of self-sacrifice among the less wealthy citizens of our town—

Aslaksen. What?

Hovstad. Self-sacrifice?

Peter Stockmann. It is pleasing evidence of a public-spirited feeling, extremely pleasing evidence. I might almost say I hardly expected it. But you have a closer knowledge of public opinion than I.

Aslaksen. But, Mr. Mayor—

Peter Stockmann. And indeed it is no small sacrifice that the town is going to make.

Hovstad. The town?

Aslaksen. But I don't understand. Is it the Baths—?

Peter Stockmann. At a provisional estimate, the alterations that the Medical Officer asserts to be desirable will cost somewhere about twenty thousand pounds.

Aslaksen. That is a lot of money, but—

Peter Stockmann. Of course it will be necessary to raise a municipal loan.

Hovstad (getting up). Surely you never mean that the town must pay—?

Aslaksen. Do you mean that it must come out of the municipal funds?—out of the ill-filled pockets of the small tradesmen?

Peter Stockmann. Well, my dear Mr. Aslaksen, where else is the money to come from?

Aslaksen. The gentlemen who own the Baths ought to provide that.

Peter Stockmann. The proprietors of the Baths are not in a position to incur any further expense.

Aslaksen. Is that absolutely certain, Mr. Mayor?

Peter Stockmann. I have satisfied myself that it is so. If the town wants these very extensive alterations, it will have to pay for them.

Aslaksen. But, damn it all—I beg your pardon—this is quite another matter, Mr. Hovstad!

Hovstad. It is, indeed.

Peter Stockmann. The most fatal part of it is that we shall be obliged to shut the Baths for a couple of years.

Hovstad. Shut them? Shut them altogether?

Aslaksen. For two years?

Peter Stockmann. Yes, the work will take as long as that—at least.

Aslaksen. I'm damned if we will stand that, Mr. Mayor! What are we householders to live upon in the meantime?

Peter Stockmann. Unfortunately, that is an extremely difficult question to answer, Mr. Aslaksen. But what would you have us do? Do you suppose we shall have a single visitor in the town, if we go about proclaiming that our water is polluted, that we are living over a plague spot, that the entire town—

Aslaksen. And the whole thing is merely imagination?

Peter Stockmann. With the best will in the world, I have not been able to come to any other conclusion.

Aslaksen. Well then I must say it is absolutely unjustifiable of Dr. Stockmann—I beg your pardon, Mr. Mayor.

Peter Stockmann. What you say is lamentably true, Mr. Aslaksen. My brother has unfortunately always been a headstrong man.

Aslaksen. After this, do you mean to give him your support, Mr. Hovstad?

Hovstad. Can you suppose for a moment that I—?

Peter Stockmann. I have drawn up a short resume of the situation as it appears from a reasonable man's point of view. In it I have indicated how certain possible defects might suitably be remedied without outrunning the resources of the Baths Committee.

Hovstad. Have you got it with you, Mr. Mayor?

Peter Stockmann (fumbling in his pocket). Yes, I brought it with me in case you should—

Aslaksen. Good Lord, there he is!

Peter Stockmann. Who? My brother?

Hovstad. Where? Where?

Aslaksen. He has just gone through the printing room.

Peter Stockmann. How unlucky! I don't want to meet him here, and I had still several things to speak to you about.

Hovstad (pointing to the door on the right). Go in there for the present.

Peter Stockmann. But—?

Hovstad. You will only find Billing in there.

Aslaksen. Quick, quick, Mr. Mayor—he is just coming.

Peter Stockmann. Yes, very well; but see that you get rid of him quickly. (Goes out through the door on the right, which ASLAKSEN opens for him and shuts after him.)

Hovstad. Pretend to be doing something, Aslaksen.

(Sits down and writes. ASLAKSEN begins foraging among a heap of newspapers that are lying on a chair.)

Dr. Stockmann (coming in from the printing room). Here I am again. (Puts down his hat and stick.)

Hovstad (writing). Already, Doctor? Hurry up with what we were speaking about, Aslaksen.

We are very pressed for time today.

Dr. Stockmann (to ASLAKSEN). No proof for me to see yet, I hear.

Aslaksen (without turning round). You couldn't expect it yet, Doctor.

Dr. Stockmann. No, no; but I am impatient, as you can understand. I shall not know a moment's peace of mind until I see it in print.

Hovstad. Hm!—It will take a good while yet, won't it, Aslaksen?

Aslaksen. Yes, I am almost afraid it will.

Dr. Stockmann. All right, my dear friends; I will come back. I do not mind coming back twice if necessary. A matter of such great importance—the welfare of the town at stake—it is no time to shirk trouble, (is just going, but stops and comes back.) Look here—there is one thing more I want to speak to you about.

Hovstad. Excuse me, but could it not wait till some other time?

Dr. Stockmann. I can tell you in half a dozen words. It is only this. When my article is read tomorrow and it is realised that I have been quietly working the whole winter for the welfare of the town—

Hovstad. Yes but, Doctor—

Dr. Stockmann. I know what you are going to say. You don't see how on earth it was any more than my duty—my obvious duty as a Citizen. Of course it wasn't; I know that as well as you. But my fellow citizens, you know—! Good Lord, think of all the good souls who think so highly of me—!

Aslaksen. Yes, our townsfolk have had a very high opinion of you so far, Doctor.

Dr. Stockmann. Yes, and that is just why I am afraid they—. Well, this is the point; when this reaches them, especially the poorer classes, and sounds in their ears like a summons to take the town's affairs into their own hands for the future...

Hovstad (getting up). Ahem! Doctor, I won't conceal from you the fact—

Dr. Stockmann. Ah I—I knew there was something in the wind! But I won't hear a word of it. If anything of that sort is being set on foot—

Hovstad. Of what sort?

Dr. Stockmann. Well, whatever it is—whether it is a demonstration in my honour, or a banquet, or a subscription list for some presentation to me—whatever it is, you most promise me solemnly and faithfully to put a stop to it. You too, Mr. Aslaksen; do you understand?

Hovstad. You must forgive me, Doctor, but sooner or later we must tell you the plain truth—

(He is interrupted by the entrance Of MRS. STOCKMANN, who comes in from the street door.)

Mrs. Stockmann (seeing her husband). Just as I thought!

Hovstad (going towards her). You too, Mrs. Stockmann?

Dr. Stockmann. What on earth do you want here, Katherine?

Mrs. Stockmann. I should think you know very well what I want.

Hovstad, Won't you sit down? Or perhaps—

Mrs. Stockmann. No, thank you; don't trouble. And you must not be offended at my coming to fetch my husband; I am the mother of three children, you know.

Dr. Stockmann. Nonsense!—we know all about that.

Mrs. Stockmann. Well, one would not give you credit for much thought for your wife and children today; if you had had that, you would not have gone and dragged us all into misfortune.

Dr. Stockmann. Are you out of your senses, Katherine! Because a man has a wife and children, is he not to be allowed to proclaim the truth-is he not to be allowed to be an actively useful citizen—is he not to be allowed to do a service to his native town!

Mrs. Stockmann. Yes, Thomas—in reason.

Aslaksen. Just what I say. Moderation in everything.

Mrs. Stockmann. And that is why you wrong us, Mr. Hovstad, in enticing my husband away from his home and making a dupe of him in all this.

Hovstad. I certainly am making a dupe of no one—

Dr. Stockmann. Making a dupe of me! Do you suppose I should allow myself to be duped!

Mrs. Stockmann. It is just what you do. I know quite well you have more brains than anyone in the town, but you are extremely easily duped, Thomas. (To Hovstad.) Please do realise that he loses his post at the Baths if you print what he has written.

Aslaksen. What!

Hovstad. Look here, Doctor!

Dr. Stockmann (laughing). Ha-ha!—just let them try! No, no—they will take good care not to. I have got the compact majority behind me, let me tell you!

Mrs. Stockmann. Yes, that is just the worst of it—your having any such horrid thing behind you.

Dr. Stockmann. Rubbish, Katherine!—Go home and look after your house and leave me to look after the community. How can you be so afraid, when I am so confident and happy? (Walks up and down, rubbing his hands.) Truth and the People will win the fight, you may be certain! I see the whole of the broad-minded middle class marching like a victorious army—! (Stops beside a chair.) What the deuce is that lying there?

Aslaksen Good Lord!

Hovstad. Ahem!

Dr. Stockmann. Here we have the topmost pinnacle of authority! (Takes the Mayor's official hat carefully between his finger-tips and holds it up in the air.)

Mrs. Stockmann. The Mayor's hat!

Dr. Stockmann. And here is the staff of office too. How in the name of all that's wonderful—?

Hovstad. Well, you see—

Dr. Stockmann. Oh, I understand. He has been here trying to talk you over. Ha-ha!—he made rather a mistake there! And as soon as he caught sight of me in the printing room. (Bursts out laughing.) Did he run away, Mr. Aslaksen?

Aslaksen (hurriedly). Yes, he ran away, Doctor.

Dr. Stockmann. Ran away without his stick or his—. Fiddlesticks! Peter doesn't run away and leave his belongings behind him. But what the deuce have you done with him? Ah!—in there, of course. Now you shall see, Katherine!

Mrs. Stockmann. Thomas—please don't—!

Aslaksen. Don't be rash, Doctor.

(DR. STOCKMANN has put on the Mayor's hat and taken his stick in his hand. He goes up to the door, opens it, and stands with his hand to his hat at the salute. PETER STOCKMANN comes in, red with anger. BILLING follows him.)

Peter Stockmann. What does this tomfoolery mean?

Dr. Stockmann. Be respectful, my good Peter. I am the chief authority in the town now. (Walks up and down.)

Mrs. Stockmann (almost in tears). Really, Thomas!

Peter Stockmann (following him about). Give me my hat and stick.

Dr. Stockmann (in the same tone as before). If you are chief constable, let me tell you that I am the Mayor—I am the master of the whole town, please understand!

Peter Stockmann. Take off my hat, I tell you. Remember it is part of an official uniform.

Dr. Stockmann. Pooh! Do you think the newly awakened lionhearted people are going to be frightened by an official hat? There is going to be a revolution in the town tomorrow, let me tell you. You thought you could turn me out; but now I shall turn you out—turn you out of all your various offices. Do you think I cannot? Listen to me. I have triumphant social forces behind me. Hovstad and Billing will thunder in the "People's Messenger," and Aslaksen will take the field at the head of the whole Householders' Association—

Aslaksen. That I won't, Doctor.

Dr. Stockmann. Of course you will—

Peter Stockmann. Ah!—may I ask then if Mr. Hovstad intends to join this agitation?

Hovstad. No, Mr. Mayor.

Aslaksen. No, Mr. Hovstad is not such a fool as to go and ruin his paper and himself for the sake of an imaginary grievance.

Dr. Stockmann (looking round him). What does this mean?

Hovstad. You have represented your case in a false light, Doctor, and therefore I am unable to give you my support.

Billing. And after what the Mayor was so kind as to tell me just now, I—

Dr. Stockmann. A false light! Leave that part of it to me. Only print my article; I am quite capable of defending it.

Hovstad. I am not going to print it. I cannot and will not and dare not print it.

Dr. Stockmann. You dare not? What nonsense!—you are the editor; and an editor controls his paper, I suppose!

Aslaksen. No, it is the subscribers, Doctor.

Peter Stockmann. Fortunately, yes.

Aslaksen. It is public opinion—the enlightened public—householders and people of that kind; they control the newspapers.

Dr. Stockmann (composedly). And I have all these influences against me?

Aslaksen. Yes, you have. It would mean the absolute ruin of the community if your article were to appear.

Dr. Stockmann. Indeed.

Peter Stockmann. My hat and stick, if you please. (DR. STOCKMANN takes off the hat and lays it on the table with the stick. PETER STOCKMANN takes them up.) Your authority as mayor has come to an untimely end.

Dr. Stockmann. We have not got to the end yet. (To Hovstad) Then it is quite impossible for you to print my article in the "People's Messenger"?

Hovstad. Quite impossible—out of regard for your family as well.

Mrs. Stockmann. You need not concern yourself about his family, thank you, Mr. Hovstad.

Peter Stockmann (taking a paper from his pocket). It will be sufficient, for the guidance of the public, if this appears. It is an official statement. May I trouble you?

Hovstad (taking the paper). Certainly; I will see that it is printed.

Dr. Stockmann. But not mine. Do you imagine that you can silence me and stifle the truth! You will not find it so easy as you suppose. Mr. Aslaksen, kindly take my manuscript at once and print it as a pamphlet—at my expense. I will have four hundred copies—no, five or six hundred.

Aslaksen. If you offered me its weight in gold, I could not lend my press for any such purpose, Doctor. It would be flying in the face of public opinion. You will not get it printed anywhere in the town.

Dr. Stockmann. Then give it me back.

Hovstad (giving him the MS.). Here it is.

Dr. Stockmann (taking his hat and stick). It shall be made public all the same. I will read it out at a mass meeting of the townspeople. All my fellow-citizens shall hear the voice of truth!

Peter Stockmann. You will not find any public body in the town that will give you the use of their hall for such a purpose.

Aslaksen. Not a single one, I am certain.

Billing. No, I'm damned if you will find one.

Mrs. Stockmann. But this is too shameful! Why should every one turn against you like that?

Dr. Stockmann (angrily). I will tell you why. It is because all the men in this town are old women—like you; they all think of nothing but their families, and never of the community.

Mrs. Stockmann (putting her arm into his). Then I will show them that an old woman can be a man for once. I am going to stand by you, Thomas!

Dr. Stockmann. Bravely said, Katherine! It shall be made public—as I am a living soul! If I can't hire a hall, I shall hire a drum, and parade the town with it and read it at every street-corner.

Peter Stockmann. You are surely not such an errant fool as that!

Dr. Stockmann. Yes, I am.

Aslaksen. You won't find a single man in the whole town to go with you.

Billing. No, I'm damned if you will.

Mrs. Stockmann. Don't give in, Thomas. I will tell the boys to go with you.

Dr. Stockmann. That is a splendid idea!

Mrs. Stockmann. Morten will be delighted; and Ejlif will do whatever he does.

Dr. Stockmann. Yes, and Petra!—and you too, Katherine!

Mrs. Stockmann. No, I won't do that; but I will stand at the window and watch you, that's what I will do.

Dr. Stockmann (puts his arms round her and kisses her). Thank you, my dear! Now you and I are going to try a fall, my fine gentlemen! I am going to see whether a pack of cowards can succeed in gagging a patriot who wants to purify society! (He and his wife go out by the street door.)

Peter Stockmann (shaking his head seriously). Now he has sent her out of her senses, too.

ACT IV

(SCENE.—A big old-fashioned room in CAPTAIN HORSTER'S house. At the back folding-doors, which are standing open, lead to an ante-room. Three windows in the left-hand wall. In the middle of the opposite wall a platform has been erected. On this is a small table with two candles, a water-bottle and glass, and a bell. The room is lit by lamps placed between the windows. In the foreground on the left there is a table with candles and a chair. To the right is a door and some chairs standing near it. The room is nearly filled with a crowd of townspeople of all sorts, a few women and schoolboys being amongst them. People are still streaming in from the back, and the room is soon filled.)

1st Citizen (meeting another). Hullo, Lamstad! You here too?

2nd Citizen. I go to every public meeting, I do.

3rd Citizen. Brought your whistle too, I expect!

2nd Citizen. I should think so. Haven't you?

3rd Citizen. Rather! And old Evensen said he was going to bring a cow-horn, he did.

2nd Citizen. Good old Evensen! (Laughter among the crowd.)

4th Citizen (coming up to them). I say, tell me what is going on here tonight?

2nd Citizen. Dr. Stockmann is going to deliver an address attacking the Mayor.

4th Citizen. But the Mayor is his brother.

1st Citizen. That doesn't matter; Dr. Stockmann's not the chap to be afraid.

3rd Citizen. But he is in the wrong; it said so in the "People's Messenger."

2nd Citizen. Yes, I expect he must be in the wrong this time, because neither the Householders' Association nor the Citizens' Club would lend him their hall for his meeting.

1st Citizen. He couldn't even get the loan of the hall at the Baths.

2nd Citizen. No, I should think not.

A Man in another part of the crowd. I say—who are we to back up in this?

Another Man, beside him. Watch Aslaksen, and do as he does.

Billing (pushing his way through the crowd, with a writing-case under his arm). Excuse me, gentlemen—do you mind letting me through? I am reporting for the "People's Messenger." Thank you very much! (He sits down at the table on the left.)

A Workman. Who was that?

Second Workman. Don't you know him? It's Billing, who writes for Aslaksen's paper.

(CAPTAIN HORSTER brings in MRS. STOCKMANN and PETRA through the door on the right. EJLIF and MORTEN follow them in.)

Horster. I thought you might all sit here; you can slip out easily from here, if things get too lively.

Mrs. Stockmann. Do you think there will be a disturbance?

Horster. One can never tell—with such a crowd. But sit down, and don't be uneasy.

Mrs. Stockmann (sitting down). It was extremely kind of you to offer my husband the room.

Horster. Well, if nobody else would—

Petra (who has sat down beside her mother). And it was a plucky thing to do, Captain Horster.

Horster. Oh, it is not such a great matter as all that.

(HOVSTAD and ASLAKSEN make their way through the crowd.)

Aslaksen (going up to HORSTER). Has the Doctor not come yet?

Horster. He is waiting in the next room. (Movement in the crowd by the door at the back.)

Hovstad. Look—here comes the Mayor!

Billing. Yes, I'm damned if he hasn't come after all!

(PETER STOCKMANN makes his way gradually through the crowd, bows courteously, and takes up a position by the wall on the left. Shortly afterwards Dr. STOCKMANN comes in by the right-hand door. He is dressed in a black frock-coat, with a white tie. There is a little feeble applause, which is hushed down. Silence is obtained.)

Dr. Stockmann (in an undertone). How do you feel, Katherine?

Mrs. Stockmann. All right, thank you. (Lowering her voice.) Be sure not to lose your temper, Thomas.

Dr. Stockmann. Oh, I know how to control myself.

(Looks at his watch, steps on to the platform, and bows. It is a quarter past—so I will begin. (Takes his MS. out of his pocket).

Aslaksen. I think we ought to elect a chairman first.

Dr. Stockmann. No, it is quite unnecessary.

Some of the Crowd. Yes—yes!

Peter Stockmann. I certainly think too that we ought to have a chairman.

Dr. Stockmann. But I have called this meeting to deliver a lecture, Peter.

Peter Stockmann. Dr. Stockmann's lecture may possibly lead to a considerable conflict of opinion.

Voices in the Crowd. A chairman! A chairman !

Hovstad. The general wish of the meeting seems to be that a chairman should be elected.

Dr. Stockmann (restraining himself). Very well—let the meeting have its way.

Aslaksen. Will the Mayor be good enough to undertake the task ?

Three Men (clapping their hands). Bravo! Bravo!

Peter Stockmann. For various reasons, which you will easily understand, I must beg to be excused. But fortunately we have amongst us a man who I think will be acceptable to you all. I refer to the President of the Householders' Association, Mr. Aslaksen.

Several voices. Yes—Aslaksen! Bravo Aslaksen!

(DR. STOCKMANN takes up his MS. and walks up and down the platform.)

Aslaksen. Since my fellow-citizens choose to entrust me with this duty, I cannot refuse.

(Loud applause. ASLAKSEN mounts the platform.)

Billing (writing), "Mr. Aslaksen was elected with enthusiasm."

Aslaksen. And now, as I am in this position, I should like to say a few brief words. I am a quiet and peaceable man, who believes in discreet moderation, and—and—in moderate discretion. All my friends can bear witness to that.

Several Voices. That's right! That's right, Aslaksen!

Aslaksen. I have learned in the school of life and experience that moderation is the most valuable virtue a citizen can possess—

Peter Stockmann. Hear, hear!

Aslaksen. —And moreover, that discretion and moderation are what enable a man to be of most service to the community. I would therefore suggest to our esteemed fellow-citizen, who has called this meeting, that he should strive to keep strictly within the bounds of moderation.

A Man by the door. Three cheers for the Moderation Society!

A Voice. Shame!

Several Voices. Sh!-Sh!

Aslaksen. No interruptions, gentlemen, please! Does anyone wish to make any remarks?

Peter Stockmann. Mr. Chairman.

Aslaksen. The Mayor will address the meeting.

Peter Stockmann. In consideration of the close relationship in which, as you all know, I stand to the present Medical Officer of the Baths, I should have preferred not to speak this evening. But my official position with regard to the Baths and my solicitude for the vital interests of the town compel me to bring forward a motion. I venture to presume that there is not a single one of our citizens present who considers it desirable that unreliable and exaggerated accounts of the sanitary condition of the Baths and the town should be spread abroad.

Several Voices. No, no! Certainly not! We protest against it!

Peter Stockmann. Therefore, I should like to propose that the meeting should not permit the Medical Officer either to read or to comment on his proposed lecture.

Dr. Stockmann (impatiently). Not permit—! What the devil—!

Mrs. Stockmann (coughing). Ahem!-ahem!

Dr. Stockmann (collecting himself). Very well, Go ahead!

Peter Stockmann. In my communication to the "People's Messenger," I have put the essential facts before the public in such a way that every fair-minded citizen can easily form his own opinion. From it you will see that the main result of the Medical Officer's proposals—apart from their constituting a vote of censure on the leading men of the town—would be to saddle the ratepayers with an unnecessary expenditure of at least some thousands of pounds.

(Sounds of disapproval among the audience, and some cat-calls.)

Aslaksen (ringing his bell). Silence, please, gentlemen! I beg to support the Mayor's motion. I quite agree with him that there is something behind this agitation started by the Doctor. He talks about the Baths; but it is a revolution he is aiming at—he wants to get the administration of the town put into new hands. No one doubts the honesty of the Doctor's intentions—no one will suggest that there can be any two opinions as to that, I myself am a believer in self-government for the people, provided it does not fall too heavily on the ratepayers. But that would be the case here; and that is why I will see Dr. Stockmann damned—I beg your pardon—before I go with him in the matter. You can pay too dearly for a thing sometimes; that is my opinion.

(Loud applause on all sides.)

Hovstad. I, too, feel called upon to explain my position. Dr. Stockmann's agitation appeared to be gaining a certain amount of sympathy at first, so I supported it as impartially as I could. But presently we had reason to suspect that we had allowed ourselves to be misled by misrepresentation of the state of affairs—

Dr. Stockmann. Misrepresentation—!

Hovstad. Well, let us say a not entirely trustworthy

representation. The Mayor's statement has proved that. I hope no one here has any doubt as to my liberal principles; the attitude of the "People's Messenger" towards important political questions is well known to everyone. But the advice of experienced and thoughtful men has convinced me that in purely local matters a newspaper ought to proceed with a certain caution.

Aslaksen. I entirely agree with the speaker.

Hovstad. And, in the matter before us, it is now an undoubted fact that Dr. Stockmann has public opinion against him. Now, what is an editor's first and most obvious duty, gentlemen? Is it not to work in harmony with his readers? Has he not received a sort of tacit mandate to work persistently and assiduously for the welfare of those whose opinions he represents? Or is it possible I am mistaken in that?

Voices from the crowd. No, no! You are quite right!

Hovstad. It has cost me a severe struggle to break with a man in whose house I have been lately a frequent guest—a man who till today has been able to pride himself on the undivided goodwill of his fellow-citizens—a man whose only, or at all events whose essential, failing is that he is swayed by his heart rather than his head.

A few scattered voices. That is true! Bravo, Stockmann!

Hovstad. But my duty to the community obliged me to break with him. And there is another consideration that impels me to oppose him, and, as far as possible, to arrest him on the perilous course he has adopted; that is, consideration for his family—

Dr. Stockmann. Please stick to the water-supply and drainage!

Hovstad. —consideration, I repeat, for his wife and his children for whom he has made no provision.

Morten. Is that us, mother?

Mrs. Stockmann. Hush!

Aslaksen. I will now put the Mayor's proposition to the vote.

Dr. Stockmann. There is no necessity! Tonight I have no intention of dealing with all that filth down at the Baths. No; I have something quite different to say to you.

Peter Stockmann (aside). What is coming now?

A Drunken Man (by the entrance door). I am a ratepayer! And therefore, I have a right to speak too! And my entire—firm—inconceivable opinion is—

A number of voices. Be quiet, at the back there!

Others. He is drunk! Turn him out! (They turn him out.)

Dr. Stockmann. Am I allowed to speak?

Aslaksen (ringing his bell). Dr. Stockmann will address the meeting.

Dr. Stockmann. I should like to have seen anyone, a few days ago, dare to attempt to silence me as has been done tonight! I would have defended my sacred rights as a man, like a lion! But now it is all one to me; I have something of even weightier importance to say to you. (The crowd presses nearer to him, MORTEN Kiil conspicuous among them.)

Dr. Stockmann (continuing). I have thought and pondered a great deal, these last few days—pondered over such a variety of things that in the end my head seemed too full to hold them—

Peter Stockmann (with a cough). Ahem!

Dr. Stockmann. —but I got them clear in my mind at last, and then I saw the whole situation lucidly. And that is why I am standing here to-night. I have a great revelation to make to you, my fellow-citizens! I will impart to you a discovery of a far wider scope than the trifling matter that our water supply is poisoned and our medicinal Baths are standing on pestiferous soil.

A number of voices (shouting). Don't talk about the Baths! We won't hear you! None of that!

Dr. Stockmann. I have already told you that what I want to speak about is the great discovery I have made lately—the discovery that all the sources of our moral life are poisoned and that the whole fabric of our civic community is founded on the pestiferous soil of falsehood.

Voices of disconcerted Citizens. What is that he says?

Peter Stockmann. Such an insinuation—!

Aslaksen (with his hand on his bell). I call upon the speaker to moderate his language.

Dr. Stockmann. I have always loved my native town as a man only can love the home of his youthful days. I was not old when I went away from here; and exile, longing and memories cast as it were an additional halo over both the town and its inhabitants. (Some clapping and applause.) And there I stayed, for many years, in a horrible hole far away up north. When I came into contact with some of the people that lived scattered about among the rocks, I often thought it would of been more service to the poor half-starved creatures if a veterinary doctor had been sent up there, instead of a man like me. (Murmurs among the crowd.)

Billing (laying down his pen). I'm damned if I have ever heard—!

Hovstad. It is an insult to a respectable population!

Dr. Stockmann. Wait a bit! I do not think anyone will charge me with having forgotten my native town up there. I was like one of the eider-ducks brooding on its nest, and what I hatched was the plans for these Baths. (Applause and protests.) And then when fate at last decreed for me the great happiness of coming home again—I assure you, gentlemen, I thought I had nothing more in the world to wish for. Or rather, there was one thing I wished for—eagerly, untiringly, ardently—and that was to be able to be of service to my native town and the good of the community.

Peter Stockmann (looking at the ceiling). You chose a strange way of doing it—ahem!

Dr. Stockmann. And so, with my eyes blinded to the real facts, I revelled in happiness. But yesterday morning—no, to be precise, it was yesterday afternoon—the eyes of my mind were opened wide, and the first thing I realised was the colossal stupidity of the authorities—. (Uproar, shouts and laughter, MRS. STOCKMANN coughs persistently.)

Peter Stockmann. Mr. Chairman!

Aslaksen (ringing his bell). By virtue of my authority—!

Dr. Stockmann. It is a petty thing to catch me up on a word, Mr. Aslaksen. What I mean is only that I got scent of the unbelievable piggishness our leading men had been responsible for down at the Baths. I can't stand leading men at any price!—I have had enough of such people in my time. They are like billy-goats on a young plantation; they do mischief everywhere. They stand in a free man's way, whichever way he turns, and what I should like best would be to see them exterminated like any other vermin—. (Uproar.)

Peter Stockmann. Mr. Chairman, can we allow such expressions to pass?

Aslaksen (with his hand on his bell). Doctor—!

Dr. Stockmann. I cannot understand how it is that I have only now acquired a clear conception of what these gentry are, when I had almost daily before my eyes in this town such an excellent specimen of them—my brother Peter—slow-witted and hide-bound in prejudice—. (Laughter, uproar and hisses. MRS. STOCKMANN Sits coughing assiduously. ASLAKSEN rings his bell violently.)

The Drunken Man (who has got in again). Is it me he is talking about? My name's Petersen, all right—but devil take me if I—

Angry Voices. Turn out that drunken man! Turn him out. (He is turned out again.)

Peter Stockmann. Who was that person?

1st Citizen. I don't know who he is, Mr. Mayor.

2nd Citizen. He doesn't belong here.

3rd Citizen. I expect he is a navvy from over at—(the rest is inaudible).

Aslaksen. He had obviously had too much beer. Proceed, Doctor; but please strive to be moderate in your language.

Dr. Stockmann. Very well, gentlemen, I will say no more about our leading men. And if anyone imagines, from what I have just said, that my object is to attack these people this evening, he is wrong—absolutely wide of the mark. For I cherish the comforting conviction that these parasites—all these venerable relics of a dying school of thought—are most admirably paving the way for their own extinction; they need no doctor's help to hasten their end. Nor is it folk of that kind who constitute the most pressing danger to the community. It is not they who are most instrumental in poisoning the sources of our moral life and infecting the ground on which we stand. It is not they who are the most dangerous enemies of truth and freedom amongst us.

Shouts from all sides. Who then? Who is it? Name! Name!

Dr. Stockmann. You may depend upon it—I shall name them! That is precisely the great discovery I made yesterday. (Raises his voice.) The most dangerous enemy of truth and freedom amongst us is the compact majority—yes, the damned compact Liberal majority—that is it! Now you know! (Tremendous uproar. Most of the crowd are shouting, stamping and hissing. Some of the older men among them exchange stolen glances and seem to be enjoying themselves. MRS. STOCKMANN gets up, looking anxious. EJLIF and MORTEN advance threateningly upon some schoolboys who are playing pranks. ASLAKSEN rings his bell and begs for silence. HOVSTAD and BILLING both talk at once, but are inaudible. At last quiet is restored.)

Aslaksen. As Chairman, I call upon the speaker to withdraw the ill-considered expressions he has just used.

Dr. Stockmann. Never, Mr. Aslaksen! It is the majority in our community that denies me my freedom and seeks to prevent my speaking the truth.

Hovstad. The majority always has right on its side.

Billing. And truth too, by God!

Dr. Stockmann. The majority never has right on its side. Never, I say! That is one of these social lies against which an independent, intelligent man must wage war. Who is it that constitute the majority of the population in a country? Is it the clever folk, or the stupid? I don't imagine you will dispute the fact that at present the stupid people are in an absolutely overwhelming majority all the world over. But, good Lord!—you can never pretend that it is right that the stupid folk should govern the clever ones! (Uproar and cries.) Oh, yes—you can shout me down, I know! But you cannot answer me. The majority has might on its side—unfortunately; but right it has not. I am in the right—I and a few other scattered individuals. The minority is always in the right. (Renewed uproar.)

Hovstad. Aha!—so Dr. Stockmann has become an aristocrat since the day before yesterday!

Dr. Stockmann. I have already said that I don't intend to waste a word on the puny, narrow-chested, short-winded crew whom we are leaving astern. Pulsating life no longer concerns itself with them. I am thinking of the few, the scattered few amongst us, who have absorbed new and vigorous truths. Such men stand, as it were, at the outposts, so far ahead that the compact majority has not yet been able to come up with them; and there they are fighting for truths that are too newly-born into the world of consciousness to have any considerable number of people on their side as yet.

Hovstad. So the Doctor is a revolutionary now!

Dr. Stockmann. Good heavens—of course I am, Mr. Hovstad! I propose to raise a revolution against the lie that the majority has the monopoly of the truth. What sort of truths are they that the majority usually supports? They are truths that are of such advanced age that they are beginning to break up. And if a truth is as old as that, it is also in a fair way to become a lie, gentlemen. (Laughter and mocking cries.) Yes, believe me or not, as you like; but truths are by no means as long-lived at Methuselah—as some folk imagine. A normally constituted truth lives, let us say, as a rule seventeen or eighteen, or at most twenty years—seldom longer. But truths as aged as that are always worn frightfully thin, and nevertheless it is only then that the majority recognises them and recommends them to the community as wholesome moral nourishment. There is no great nutritive value in that sort of fare, I can assure you; and, as a doctor, I ought to know. These "majority truths" are like last year's cured meat—like rancid, tainted ham; and they are the origin of the moral scurvy that is rampant in our communities.

Aslaksen. It appears to me that the speaker is wandering a long way from his subject.

Peter Stockmann. I quite agree with the Chairman.

Dr. Stockmann. Have you gone clean out of your senses, Peter? I am sticking as closely to my subject as I can; for my subject is precisely this, that it is the masses, the majority—this infernal compact majority—that poisons the sources of our moral life and infects the ground we stand on.

Hovstad. And all this because the great, broadminded majority of the people is prudent enough to show deference only to well-ascertained and well-approved truths?

Dr. Stockmann. Ah, my good Mr. Hovstad, don't talk nonsense about well-ascertained truths! The truths of which the masses now approve are the very truths that the fighters at the outposts held to in the days of our grandfathers. We fighters at the outposts nowadays no longer approve of them; and I do not believe there is any other well-ascertained truth except this, that no community can live a healthy life if it is nourished only on such old marrowless truths.

Hovstad. But, instead of standing there using vague generalities, it would be interesting if you would tell us what these old marrowless truths are, that we are nourished on.

(Applause from many quarters.)

Dr. Stockmann. Oh, I could give you a whole string of such abominations; but to begin with I will confine myself to one well-approved truth, which at bottom is a foul lie, but upon which nevertheless Mr. Hovstad and the "People's Messenger" and all the "Messenger's" supporters are nourished.

Hovstad. And that is—?

Dr. Stockmann. That is, the doctrine you have inherited from your forefathers and proclaim thoughtlessly far and wide—the doctrine that the public, the crowd, the masses, are the essential part of the population—that they constitute the People—that the common folk, the ignorant and incomplete element in the community, have the same right to pronounce judgment and to approve, to direct and to govern, as the isolated, intellectually superior personalities in it.

Billing. Well, damn me if ever I—

Hovstad (at the same time, shouting out). Fellow-citizens, take good note of that!

A number of voices (angrily). Oho!—we are not the People! Only the superior folk are to govern, are they!

A Workman. Turn the fellow out for talking such rubbish!

Another. Out with him!

Another (calling out). Blow your horn, Evensen!

(A horn is blown loudly, amidst hisses and an angry uproar.)

Dr. Stockmann (when the noise has somewhat abated). Be reasonable! Can't you stand hearing the voice of truth for once? I don't in the least expect you to agree with me all at once; but I must say I did expect Mr. Hovstad to admit I was right, when he had recovered his composure a little. He claims to be a freethinker—

Voices (in murmurs of astonishment). Freethinker, did he say? Is Hovstad a freethinker?

Hovstad (shouting). Prove it, Dr. Stockmann! When have I said so in print?

Dr. Stockmann (reflecting). No, confound it, you are right!—you have never had the courage to. Well, I won't put you in a hole, Mr. Hovstad. Let us say it is I that am the freethinker, then. I am going to prove to you, scientifically, that the "People's Messenger" leads you by the nose in a shameful manner when it tells you that you—that the common people, the crowd, the masses, are the real essence of the People. That is only a newspaper lie, I tell you! The common people are nothing more than the raw material of which a People is made. (Groans, laughter and uproar.) Well, isn't that the case? Isn't there an enormous difference between a well-bred and an ill-bred strain of animals? Take, for instance, a common barn-door hen. What sort of eating do you get from a shrivelled up old scrag of a fowl like that? Not much, do you! And what sort of eggs does it lay? A fairly good crow or a raven can lay pretty nearly as good an egg. But take a well-bred Spanish or Japanese hen, or a good pheasant or a turkey—then you will see the difference. Or take the case of dogs, with whom we humans are on such intimate terms. Think first of an ordinary common cur—I mean one of the horrible, coarse-haired, low-bred curs that do nothing but run about the streets and befoul the walls of the houses. Compare one of these curs with a poodle whose sires for many generations have been bred in a gentleman's house, where they have had the best of food and had the opportunity of hearing soft voices and music. Do you not think that the poodle's brain is developed to quite a different degree from that of the cur? Of course it is. It is puppies of well-bred poodles like that, that showmen train to do incredibly clever tricks—things that a common cur could never learn to do even if it stood on its head. (Uproar and mocking cries.)

A Citizen (calls out). Are you going to make out we are dogs, now?

Another Citizen. We are not animals, Doctor!

Dr. Stockmann. Yes but, bless my soul, we are, my friend! It is true we are the finest animals anyone could wish for; but, even among us, exceptionally fine animals are rare. There is a tremendous difference between poodle-men and cur-men. And the amusing part of it is, that Mr. Hovstad quite agrees with me as long as it is a question of four-footed animals—

Hovstad. Yes, it is true enough as far as they are concerned.

Dr. Stockmann. Very well. But as soon as I extend the principle and apply it to two-legged animals, Mr. Hovstad stops short. He no longer dares to think independently, or to pursue his ideas to their logical conclusion; so, he turns the whole theory upside down and proclaims in the "People's Messenger" that it is the barn-door hens and street curs that are the finest specimens in the menagerie. But that is always the way, as long as a man retains the traces of common origin and has not worked his way up to intellectual distinction.

Hovstad. I lay no claim to any sort of distinction, I am the son of humble country-folk, and I am proud that the stock I come from is rooted deep among the common people he insults.

Voices. Bravo, Hovstad! Bravo! Bravo!

Dr. Stockmann. The kind of common people I mean are not only to be found low down in the social scale; they crawl and swarm all around us—even in the highest social positions. You have only to look at your own fine, distinguished Mayor! My brother Peter is every bit as plebeian as anyone that walks in two shoes— (laughter and hisses)

Peter Stockmann. I protest against personal allusions of this kind.

Dr. Stockmann (imperturbably).—and that, not because he is like myself, descended from some old rascal of a pirate from Pomerania or thereabouts—because that is who we are descended from—

Peter Stockmann. An absurd legend. I deny it!

Dr. Stockmann. —but because he thinks what his superiors think, and holds the same opinions as they, People who do that are, intellectually speaking, common people; and, that is why my magnificent brother Peter is in reality so very far from any distinction—and consequently also so far from being liberal-minded.

Peter Stockmann. Mr. Chairman—!

Hovstad. So it is only the distinguished men that are liberal-minded in this country? We are learning something quite new! (Laughter.)

Dr. Stockmann. Yes, that is part of my new discovery too. And another part of it is that broad-mindedness is almost precisely the same thing as morality. That is why I maintain that it is absolutely inexcusable in the "People's Messenger" to proclaim, day in and day out, the false doctrine that it is the masses, the crowd, the compact majority, that have the monopoly of broad-mindedness and morality—and that vice and corruption and every kind of intellectual depravity are the result of culture, just as all the filth that is draining into our Baths is the result of the tanneries up at Molledal! (Uproar and interruptions. DR. STOCKMANN is undisturbed, and goes on, carried away by his ardour, with a smile.) And yet this same "People's Messenger" can go on preaching that the masses ought to be elevated to higher conditions of life! But, bless my soul, if the "Messenger's" teaching is to be depended upon, this very raising up the masses would mean nothing more or less than setting them straightway upon the paths of depravity! Happily the theory that culture demoralises is only an old falsehood that our forefathers believed in and we have inherited. No, it is ignorance, poverty, ugly conditions of life, that do the devil's work! In a house which does not get aired and swept every day—my wife Katherine maintains that the floor ought to be scrubbed as well, but that is a debatable question—in such a house, let me tell you, people will lose within two or three years the power of thinking or acting in a moral manner. Lack of oxygen weakens the conscience. And there must be a plentiful lack of oxygen in very many houses in this town, I should think, judging from the fact that the whole compact majority can be unconscientious enough to wish to build the town's prosperity on a quagmire of falsehood and deceit.

Aslaksen. We cannot allow such a grave accusation to be flung at a citizen community.

A Citizen. I move that the Chairman direct the speaker to sit down.

Voices (angrily). Hear, hear! Quite right! Make him sit down!

Dr. Stockmann (losing his self-control). Then I will go and shout the truth at every street corner! I will write it in other towns' newspapers! The whole country shall know what is going on here!

Hovstad. It almost seems as if Dr. Stockmann's intention were to ruin the town.

Dr. Stockmann. Yes, my native town is so dear to me that I would rather ruin it than see it flourishing upon a lie.

Aslaksen. This is really serious. (Uproar and cat-calls MRS. STOCKMANN coughs, but to no purpose; her husband does not listen to her any longer.)

Hovstad (shouting above the din). A man must be a public enemy to wish to ruin a whole community!

Dr. Stockmann (with growing fervor). What does the destruction of a community matter, if it lives on lies? It ought to be razed to the ground. I tell you— All who live by lies ought to be exterminated like vermin! You will end by infecting the whole country; you will bring about such a state of things that the whole country will deserve to be ruined. And if things come to that pass, I shall say from the bottom of my heart: Let the whole country perish, let all these people be exterminated!

Voices from the crowd. That is talking like an out-and-out enemy of the people!

Billing. There sounded the voice of the people, by all that's holy!

The whole crowd (shouting). Yes, yes! He is an enemy of the people! He hates his country! He hates his own people!

Aslaksen. Both as a citizen and as an individual, I am profoundly disturbed by what we have had to listen to. Dr. Stockmann has shown himself in a light I should never have dreamed of. I am unhappily obliged to subscribe to the opinion which I have just heard my estimable fellow-citizens utter; and I propose that we should give expression to that opinion in a resolution. I propose a resolution as follows: "This meeting declares that it considers Dr. Thomas Stockmann, Medical Officer of the Baths, to be an enemy of the people." (A storm of cheers and applause. A number of men surround the DOCTOR and hiss him. MRS. STOCKMANN and PETRA have got up from their seats. MORTEN and EJLIF are fighting the other schoolboys for hissing; some of their elders separate them.)

Dr. Stockmann (to the men who are hissing him). Oh, you fools! I tell you that—

Aslaksen (ringing his bell). We cannot hear you now, Doctor. A formal vote is about to be taken; but, out of regard for personal feelings, it shall be by ballot and not verbal. Have you any clean paper, Mr. Billing?

Billing. I have both blue and white here.

Aslaksen (going to him). That will do nicely; we shall get on more quickly that way. Cut it up into small strips—yes, that's it. (To the meeting.) Blue means no; white means yes. I will come round myself and collect votes. (PETER STOCKMANN leaves the hall. ASLAKSEN and one or two others go round the room with the slips of paper in their hats.)

1st Citizen (to HOVSTAD). I say, what has come to the Doctor? What are we to think of it?

Hovstad. Oh, you know how headstrong he is.

2nd Citizen (to BILLING). Billing, you go to their house—have you ever noticed if the fellow drinks?

Billing. Well I'm hanged if I know what to say. There are always spirits on the table when you go.

3rd Citizen. I rather think he goes quite off his head sometimes.

1st Citizen. I wonder if there is any madness in his family?

Billing. I shouldn't wonder if there were.

4th Citizen. No, it is nothing more than sheer malice; he wants to get even with somebody for something or other.

Billing. Well certainly he suggested a rise in his salary on one occasion lately, and did not get it.

The Citizens (together). Ah!—then it is easy to understand how it is!

The Drunken Man (who has got among the audience again). I want a blue one, I do! And I want a white one too!

Voices. It's that drunken chap again! Turn him out!

Morten Kiil. (going up to DR. STOCKMANN). Well, Stockmann, do you see what these monkey tricks of yours lead to?

Dr. Stockmann. I have done my duty.

Morten Kiil. What was that you said about the tanneries at Molledal?

Dr. Stockmann. You heard well enough. I said they were the source of all the filth.

Morten Kiil. My tannery too?

Dr. Stockmann. Unfortunately your tannery is by far the worst.

Morten Kiil. Are you going to put that in the papers?

Dr. Stockmann. I shall conceal nothing.

Morten Kiil. That may cost you dearly, Stockmann. (Goes out.)

A Stout Man (going UP to CAPTAIN HORSTER, Without taking any notice of the ladies). Well, Captain, so you lend your house to enemies of the people?

Horster. I imagine I can do what I like with my own possessions, Mr. Vik.

The Stout Man. Then you can have no objection to my doing the same with mine.

Horster. What do you mean, sir?

The Stout Man. You shall hear from me in the morning. (Turns his back on him and moves off.)

Petra. Was that not your owner, Captain Horster?

Horster. Yes, that was Mr. Vik the shipowner.

Aslaksen (with the voting-papers in his hands, gets up on to the platform and rings his bell). Gentlemen, allow me to announce the result. By the votes of every one here except one person—

A Young Man. That is the drunk chap!

Aslaksen. By the votes of everyone here except a tipsy man, this meeting of citizens declares Dr. Thomas Stockmann to be an enemy of the people. (Shouts and applause.) Three cheers for our ancient and honourable citizen community! (Renewed applause.) Three cheers for our able and energetic Mayor, who has so loyally suppressed the promptings of family feeling! (Cheers.) The meeting is dissolved. (Gets down.)

Billing. Three cheers for the Chairman!

The whole crowd. Three cheers for Aslaksen! Hurrah!

Dr. Stockmann. My hat and coat, Petra! Captain, have you room on your ship for passengers to the

New World?

Horster. For you and yours we will make room, Doctor.

Dr. Stockmann (as PETRA helps him into his coat), Good. Come, Katherine! Come, boys!

Mrs. Stockmann (in an undertone). Thomas, dear, let us go out by the back way.

Dr. Stockmann. No back ways for me, Katherine, (Raising his voice.) You will hear more of this enemy of the people, before he shakes the dust off his shoes upon you! I am not so forgiving as a certain Person; I do not say: "I forgive you, for ye know not what ye do."

Aslaksen (shouting). That is a blasphemous comparison, Dr. Stockmann!

Billing. It is, by God! It's dreadful for an earnest man to listen to.

A Coarse Voice. Threatens us now, does he!

Other Voices (excitedly). Let's go and break his windows! Duck him in the fjord!

Another Voice. Blow your horn, Evensen! Pip, pip!

(Horn-blowing, hisses, and wild cries. DR. STOCKMANN goes out through the hall with his family, HORSTER elbowing a way for them.)

The Whole Crowd (howling after them as they go). Enemy of the People! Enemy of the People!

Billing (as he puts his papers together). Well, I'm damned if I go and drink toddy with the Stockmanns tonight!

(The crowd press towards the exit. The uproar continues outside; shouts of "Enemy of the People!" are heard from without.)

ACT V

(SCENE.—DR. STOCKMANN'S study. Bookcases and cabinets containing specimens, line the walls. At the back is a door leading to the hall; in the foreground on the left, a door leading to the sitting-room. In the righthand wall are two windows, of which all the panes are broken. The DOCTOR'S desk, littered with books and papers, stands in the middle of the room, which is in disorder. It is morning. DR. STOCKMANN in dressing-gown, slippers and a smoking-cap, is bending down and raking with an umbrella under one of the cabinets. After a little while he rakes out a stone.)

Dr. Stockmann (calling through the open sitting-room door). Katherine, I have found another one.

Mrs. Stockmann (from the sitting-room). Oh, you will find a lot more yet, I expect.

Dr. Stockmann (adding the stone to a heap of others on the table). I shall treasure these stones as relics. Ejlif and Morten shall look at them every day, and when they are grown up they shall inherit them as heirlooms. (Rakes about under a bookcase.) Hasn't—what the deuce is her name?—the girl, you know—hasn't she been to fetch the glazier yet?

Mrs. Stockmann (coming in). Yes, but he said he didn't know if he would be able to come today.

Dr. Stockmann. You will see he won't dare to come.

Mrs. Stockmann. Well, that is just what Randine thought—that he didn't dare to, on account of the neighbours. (Calls into the sitting-room.) What is it you want, Randine? Give it to me. (Goes in, and comes out again directly.) Here is a letter for you, Thomas.

Dr. Stockmann. Let me see it. (Opens and reads it.) Ah!—of course.

Mrs. Stockmann. Who is it from?

Dr. Stockmann. From the landlord. Notice to quit.

Mrs. Stockmann. Is it possible? Such a nice man

Dr. Stockmann (looking at the letter). Does not dare do otherwise, he says. Doesn't like doing it, but dare not do otherwise—on account of his fellow-citizens—out of regard for public opinion. Is in a dependent position—dares not offend certain influential men.

Mrs. Stockmann. There, you see, Thomas!

Dr. Stockmann. Yes, yes, I see well enough; the whole lot of them in the town are cowards; not a man among them dares do anything for fear of the others. (Throws the letter on to the table.) But it doesn't matter to us, Katherine. We are going to sail away to the New World, and—

Mrs. Stockmann. But, Thomas, are you sure we are well advised to take this step?

Dr. Stockmann. Are you suggesting that I should stay here, where they have pilloried me as an enemy of the people—branded me—broken my windows! And just look here, Katherine—they have torn a great rent in my black trousers too!

Mrs. Stockmann. Oh, dear!—and they are the best pair you have got!

Dr. Stockmann. You should never wear your best trousers

when you go out to fight for freedom and truth. It is not that I care so much about the trousers, you know; you can always sew them up again for me. But that the common herd should dare to make this attack on me, as if they were my equals—that is what I cannot, for the life of me, swallow!

Mrs. Stockmann. There is no doubt they have behaved very ill toward you, Thomas; but is that sufficient reason for our leaving our native country for good and all?

Dr. Stockmann. If we went to another town, do you suppose we should not find the common people just as insolent as they are here? Depend upon it, there is not much to choose between them. Oh, well, let the curs snap—that is not the worst part of it. The worst is that, from one end of this country to the other, every man is the slave of his Party. Although, as far as that goes, I daresay it is not much better in the free West either; the compact majority, and liberal public opinion, and all that infernal old bag of tricks are probably rampant there too. But there things are done on a larger scale, you see. They may kill you, but they won't put you to death by slow torture. They don't squeeze a free man's soul in a vice, as they do here. And, if need be, one can live in solitude. (Walks up and down.) If only I knew where there was a virgin forest or a small South Sea island for sale, cheap—

Mrs. Stockmann. But think of the boys, Thomas!

Dr. Stockmann (standing still). What a strange woman you are, Katherine! Would you prefer to have the boys grow up in a society like this? You saw for yourself last night that half the population are out of their minds; and if the other half have not lost their senses, it is because they are mere brutes, with no sense to lose.

Mrs. Stockmann. But, Thomas dear, the imprudent things you said had something to do with it, you know.

Dr. Stockmann. Well, isn't what I said perfectly true? Don't they turn every idea topsy-turvy? Don't they make a regular hotchpotch of right and wrong? Don't they say that the things I know are true, are lies? The craziest part of it all is the fact of these "liberals," men of full age, going about in crowds imagining that they are the broad-minded party! Did you ever hear anything like it, Katherine!

Mrs. Stockmann. Yes, yes, it's mad enough of them, certainly; but—(PETRA comes in from the sitting-room). Back from school already?

Petra. Yes. I have been given notice of dismissal.

Mrs. Stockmann. Dismissal?

Dr. Stockmann. You too?

Petra. Mrs. Busk gave me my notice; so I thought it was best to go at once.

Dr. Stockmann. You were perfectly right, too!

Mrs. Stockmann. Who would have thought Mrs. Busk was a woman like that!

Petra. Mrs. Busk isn't a bit like that, mother; I saw quite plainly how it hurt her to do it. But she didn't dare do otherwise, she said; and so I got my notice.

Dr. Stockmann (laughing and rubbing his hands). She didn't dare do otherwise, either! It's delicious!

Mrs. Stockmann. Well, after the dreadful scenes last night—

Petra. It was not only that. Just listen to this, father!

Dr. Stockmann. Well?

Petra. Mrs. Busk showed me no less than three letters she received this morning—

Dr. Stockmann. Anonymous, I suppose?

Petra. Yes.

Dr. Stockmann. Yes, because they didn't dare to risk signing their names, Katherine!

Petra. And two of them were to the effect that a man, who has been our guest here, was declaring last night at the Club that my views on various subjects are extremely emancipated—

Dr. Stockmann. You did not deny that, I hope?

Petra. No, you know I wouldn't. Mrs. Busk's own views are tolerably emancipated, when we are alone together; but now that this report about me is being spread, she dare not keep me on any longer.

Mrs. Stockmann. And someone who had been a guest of ours! That shows you the return you get for your hospitality, Thomas!

Dr. Stockmann. We won't live in such a disgusting hole any longer. Pack up as quickly as you can, Katherine; the sooner we can get away, the better.

Mrs. Stockmann. Be quiet—I think I hear someone in the hall. See who it is, Petra.

Petra (opening the door). Oh, it's you, Captain Horster! Do come in.

Horster (coming in). Good morning. I thought I would just come in and see how you were.

Dr. Stockmann (shaking his hand). Thanks—that is really kind of you.

Mrs. Stockmann. And thank you, too, for helping us through the crowd, Captain Horster.

Petra. How did you manage to get home again?

Horster. Oh, somehow or other. I am fairly strong,

and there is more sound than fury about these folk.

Dr. Stockmann. Yes, isn't their swinish cowardice astonishing? Look here, I will show you something! There are all the stones they have thrown through my windows. Just look at them! I'm hanged if there are more than two decently large bits of hard stone in the whole heap; the rest are nothing but gravel—wretched little things. And yet they stood out there bawling and swearing that they would do me some violence; but as for doing anything—you don't see much of that in this town.

Horster. Just as well for you this time, doctor!

Dr. Stockmann. True enough. But it makes one angry all the same; because if some day it should be a question of a national fight in real earnest, you will see that public opinion will be in favour of taking to one's heels, and the compact majority will turn tail like a flock of sheep, Captain Horster. That is what is so mournful to think of; it gives me so much concern, that—. No, devil take it, it is ridiculous to care about it! They have called me an enemy of the people, so an enemy of the people let me be!

Mrs. Stockmann. You will never be that, Thomas.

Dr. Stockmann. Don't swear to that, Katherine. To be called an ugly name may have the same effect as a pin-scratch in the lung. And that hateful name—I can't get quit of it. It is sticking here in the pit of my stomach, eating into me like a corrosive acid. And no magnesia will remove it.

Petra. Bah!—you should only laugh at them, father,

Horster. They will change their minds some day,

Doctor.

Mrs. Stockmann. Yes, Thomas, as sure as you are standing here.

Dr. Stockmann. Perhaps, when it is too late. Much good may it do them! They may wallow in their filth then and rue the day when they drove a patriot into exile. When do you sail, Captain Horster?

Horster. Hm!—that was just what I had come to speak about—

Dr. Stockmann. Why, has anything gone wrong with the ship?

Horster. No; but what has happened is that I am not to sail in it.

Petra. Do you mean that you have been dismissed from your command?

Horster (smiling). Yes, that's just it.

Petra. You too.

Mrs. Stockmann. There, you see, Thomas!

Dr. Stockmann. And that for the truth's sake! Oh, if I had thought such a thing possible—

Horster. You mustn't take it to heart; I shall be sure to find a job with some ship-owner or other, elsewhere.

Dr. Stockmann. And that is this man Vik—a wealthy man, independent of everyone and everything—! Shame on him!

Horster. He is quite an excellent fellow otherwise; he told me himself he would willingly have kept me on, if only he had dared—

Dr. Stockmann. But he didn't dare? No, of course not.

Horster. It is not such an easy matter, he said, for a party man—

Dr. Stockmann. The worthy man spoke the truth. A party is like a sausage machine; it mashes up all sorts of heads together into the same mincemeat—fatheads and blockheads, all in one mash!

Mrs. Stockmann. Come, come, Thomas dear!

Petra (to HORSTER). If only you had not come home with us, things might not have come to this pass.

Horster. I do not regret it.

Petra (holding out her hand to him). Thank you for that!

Horster (to DR. STOCKMANN). And so what I came to say was that if you are determined to go away, I have thought of another plan—

Dr. Stockmann. That's splendid!—if only we can get away at once.

Mrs. Stockmann. Hush!—wasn't that some one knocking?

Petra. That is uncle, surely.

Dr. Stockmann. Aha! (Calls out.) Come in!

Mrs. Stockmann. Dear Thomas, promise me definitely—. (PETER STOCKMANN comes in from the hall.)

Peter Stockmann. Oh, you are engaged. In that case, I will—

Dr. Stockmann. No, no, come in.

Peter Stockmann. But I wanted to speak to you alone.

Mrs. Stockmann. We will go into the sitting-room in the meanwhile.

Horster. And I will look in again later.

Dr. Stockmann. No, go in there with them, Captain Horster; I want to hear more about—.

Horster. Very well, I will wait, then. (He follows MRS. STOCKMANN and PETRA into the sitting-room.)

Dr. Stockmann. I daresay you find it rather draughty here today. Put your hat on.

Peter Stockmann. Thank you, if I may. (Does so.) I think I

caught cold last night; I stood and shivered—

Dr. Stockmann. Really? I found it warm enough.

Peter Stockmann. I regret that it was not in my power to prevent those excesses last night.

Dr. Stockmann. Have you anything in particular to say to me besides that?

Peter Stockmann (taking a big letter from his pocket). I have this document for you, from the Baths Committee.

Dr. Stockmann. My dismissal?

Peter Stockmann. Yes, dating from today. (Lays the letter on the table.) It gives us pain to do it; but, to speak frankly, we dared not do otherwise on account of public opinion.

Dr. Stockmann (smiling). Dared not? I seem to have heard that word before, today.

Peter Stockmann. I must beg you to understand your position clearly. For the future you must not count on any practice whatever in the town.

Dr. Stockmann. Devil take the practice! But why are you so sure of that?

Peter Stockmann. The Householders' Association is circulating a list from house to house. All right-minded citizens are being called upon to give up employing you; and I can assure you that not a single head of a family will risk refusing his signature. They simply dare not.

Dr. Stockmann. No, no; I don't doubt it. But what then?

Peter Stockmann. If I might advise you, it would be best to leave the place for a little while—

Dr. Stockmann. Yes, the propriety of leaving the place has occurred to me.

Peter Stockmann. Good. And then, when you have had six months to think things over, if, after mature consideration, you can persuade yourself to write a few words of regret, acknowledging your error—

Dr. Stockmann. I might have my appointment restored to me, do you mean?

Peter Stockmann. Perhaps. It is not at all impossible.

Dr. Stockmann. But what about public opinion, then? Surely you would not dare to do it on account of public feeling...

Peter Stockmann. Public opinion is an extremely mutable thing. And, to be quite candid with you, it is a matter of great importance to us to have some admission of that sort from you in writing.

Dr. Stockmann. Oh, that's what you are after, is it! I will just trouble you to remember what I said to you lately about foxy tricks of that sort!

Peter Stockmann. Your position was quite different then. At that time you had reason to suppose you had the whole town at your back—

Dr. Stockmann. Yes, and now I feel I have the whole town ON my back—(flaring up). I would not do it if I had the devil and his dam on my back—! Never—never, I tell you!

Peter Stockmann. A man with a family has no right to behave as you do. You have no right to do it, Thomas.

Dr. Stockmann. I have no right! There is only one single thing in the world a free man has no right to do. Do you know what that is?

Peter Stockmann. No.

Dr. Stockmann. Of course you don't, but I will tell you. A free man has no right to soil himself with filth; he has no right to behave in a way that would justify his spitting in his own face.

Peter Stockmann. This sort of thing sounds extremely plausible, of course; and if there were no other explanation for your obstinacy—. But as it happens that there is.

Dr. Stockmann. What do you mean?

Peter Stockmann. You understand, very well what I mean. But, as your brother and as a man of discretion, I advise you not to build too much upon expectations and prospects that may so very easily fail you.

Dr. Stockmann. What in the world is all this about?

Peter Stockmann. Do you really ask me to believe that you are ignorant of the terms of Mr. Kiil's will?

Dr. Stockmann. I know that the small amount he possesses is to go to an institution for indigent old workpeople. How does that concern me?

Peter Stockmann. In the first place, it is by no means a small amount that is in question. Mr. Kiil is a fairly wealthy man.

Dr. Stockmann. I had no notion of that!

Peter Stockmann. Hm!—hadn't you really? Then I suppose you had no notion, either, that a considerable portion of his wealth will come to your children, you and your wife having a liferent of the capital. Has he never told you so?

Dr. Stockmann. Never, on my honour! Quite the reverse; he has consistently done nothing but fume at being so unconscionably heavily taxed. But are you perfectly certain of this, Peter?

Peter Stockmann. I have it from an absolutely reliable source.

Dr. Stockmann. Then, thank God, Katherine is provided for—and the children too! I must tell her this at once—(calls out) Katherine, Katherine!

Peter Stockmann (restraining him). Hush, don't say a word yet!

Mrs. Stockmann (opening the door). What is the matter?

Dr. Stockmann. Oh, nothing, nothing; you can go back. (She shuts the door. DR. STOCKMANN walks up and down in his excitement.) Provided for!—Just think of it, we are all provided for! And for life! What a blessed feeling it is to know one is provided for!

Peter Stockmann. Yes, but that is just exactly what you are not. Mr. Kiil can alter his will any day he likes.

Dr. Stockmann. But he won't do that, my dear Peter. The "Badger" is much too delighted at my attack on you and your wise friends.

Peter Stockmann (starts and looks intently at him). Ah, that throws a light on various things.

Dr. Stockmann. What things?

Peter Stockmann. I see that the whole thing was a combined manoeuvre on your part and his. These violent, reckless attacks that you have made against the leading men of the town, under the pretence that it was in the name of truth—

Dr. Stockmann. What about them?

Peter Stockmann. I see that they were nothing else than the stipulated price for that vindictive old man's will.

Dr. Stockmann (almost speechless). Peter—you are the most disgusting plebeian I have ever met in all my life.

Peter Stockmann. All is over between us. Your dismissal is irrevocable—we have a weapon against you now. (Goes out.)

Dr. Stockmann. For shame! For shame! (Calls out.) Katherine, you must have the floor scrubbed after him! Let—what's her name—devil take it, the girl who has always got soot on her nose—

Mrs. Stockmann. (in the sitting-room). Hush, Thomas, be quiet!

Petra (coming to the door). Father, grandfather is here, asking if he may speak to you alone.

Dr. Stockmann. Certainly he may. (Going to the door.) Come in, Mr. Kiil. (MORTEN KIIL comes in. DR. STOCKMANN shuts the door after him.) What can I do for you? Won't you sit down?

Morten Kiil. I won't sit. (Looks around.) You look very comfortable here today, Thomas.

Dr. Stockmann. Yes, don't we!

Morten Kiil. Very comfortable—plenty of fresh air. I should think you have got enough to-day of that oxygen you were talking about yesterday. Your conscience must be in splendid order to-day, I should think.

Dr. Stockmann. It is.

Morten Kiil. So I should think. (Taps his chest.) Do you know what I have got here?

Dr. Stockmann. A good conscience, too, I hope.

Morten Kiil. Bah!—No, it is something better than that. (He takes a thick pocket-book from his breast-pocket, opens it, and displays a packet of papers.)

Dr. Stockmann (looking at him in astonishment). Shares in the Baths?

Morten Kiil. They were not difficult to get today.

Dr. Stockmann. And you have been buying—?

Morten Kiil. As many as I could pay for.

Dr. Stockmann. But, my dear Mr. Kiil—consider the state of the Baths' affairs!

Morten Kiil. If you behave like a reasonable man, you can soon set the Baths on their feet again.

Dr. Stockmann. Well, you can see for yourself that I have done all I can, but—. They are all mad in this town!

Morten Kiil. You said yesterday that the worst of this pollution came from my tannery. If that is true, then my grandfather and my father before me, and I myself, for many years past, have been poisoning the town like three destroying angels. Do you think I am going to sit quiet under that reproach?

Dr. Stockmann. Unfortunately I am afraid you will have to.

Morten Kiil. No, thank you. I am jealous of my name and reputation. They call me "the Badger," I am told. A badger is a kind of pig, I believe; but I am not going to give them the right to call me that. I mean to live and die a clean man.

Dr. Stockmann. And how are you going to set about it?

Morten Kiil. You shall cleanse me, Thomas.

Dr. Stockmann. I!

Morten Kiil. Do you know what money I have bought these shares with? No, of course you can't know—but I will tell you. It is the money that Katherine and Petra and the boys will have when I am gone. Because I have been able to save a little bit after all, you know.

Dr. Stockmann (flaring up). And you have gone and taken Katherine's money for this!

Morten Kiil. Yes, the whole of the money is invested in the Baths now. And now I just want to see whether you are quite stark, staring mad, Thomas! If you still make out that these animals and other nasty things of that sort come from my tannery, it will be exactly as if you were to flay broad strips of skin from Katherine's body, and Petra's, and the boys'; and no decent man would do that—unless he were mad.

Dr. Stockmann (walking up and down). Yes, but I am mad; I am mad!

Morten Kiil. You cannot be so absurdly mad as all that, when it is a question of your wife and children.

Dr. Stockmann (standing still in front of him). Why couldn't you consult me about it, before you went and bought all that trash?

Morten Kiil. What is done cannot be undone.

Dr. Stockmann (walks about uneasily). If only I were not so certain about it—! But I am absolutely convinced that I am right.

Morten Kiil (weighing the pocket-book in his hand). If you stick to your mad idea, this won't be worth much, you know. (Puts the pocket-book in his pocket.)

Dr. Stockmann. But, hang it all! It might be possible for science to discover some prophylactic, I should think—or some antidote of some kind—

Morten Kiil. To kill these animals, do you mean?

Dr. Stockmann. Yes, or to make them innocuous.

Morten Kiil. Couldn't you try some rat's-bane?

Dr. Stockmann. Don't talk nonsense! They all say it is only imagination, you know. Well, let it go at that! Let them have their own way about it! Haven't the ignorant, narrow-minded curs reviled me as an enemy of the people?—and haven't they been ready to tear the clothes off my back too?

Morten Kiil. And broken all your windows to pieces!

Dr. Stockmann. And then there is my duty to my family. I must talk it over with Katherine; she is great on those things.

Morten Kiil. That is right; be guided by a reasonable woman's advice.

Dr. Stockmann (advancing towards him). To think you could do such a preposterous thing! Risking Katherine's money in this way, and putting me in such a horribly painful dilemma! When I look at you, I think I see the devil himself—.

Morten Kiil. Then I had better go. But I must have an answer from you before two o'clock—yes or no. If it is no, the shares go to a charity, and that this very day.

Dr. Stockmann. And what does Katherine get?

Morten Kiil. Not a halfpenny. (The door leading to the hall opens, and HOVSTAD and ASLAKSEN make their appearance.) Look at those two!

Dr. Stockmann (staring at them). What the devil!—have YOU actually the face to come into my house?

Hovstad. Certainly.

Aslaksen. We have something to say to you, you see.

Morten Kiil (in a whisper). Yes or no—before two o'clock.

Aslaksen (glancing at HOVSTAD). Aha! (MORTEN KIIL goes out.)

Dr. Stockmann. Well, what do you want with me? Be brief.

Hovstad. I can quite understand that you are annoyed with us for our attitude at the meeting yesterday.

Dr. Stockmann. Attitude, do you call it? Yes, it was a charming attitude! I call it weak, womanish—damnably shameful!

Hovstad. Call it what you like, we could not do otherwise.

Dr. Stockmann. You DARED not do otherwise—isn't that it?

Hovstad. Well, if you like to put it that way.

Aslaksen. But why did you not let us have word of it beforehand?—just a hint to Mr. Hovstad or to me?

Dr. Stockmann. A hint? Of what?

Aslaksen. Of what was behind it all.

Dr. Stockmann. I don't understand you in the least—

Aslaksen (with a confidential nod). Oh yes, you do, Dr. Stockmann.

Hovstad. It is no good making a mystery of it any longer.

Dr. Stockmann (looking first at one of them and then at the other). What the devil do you both mean?

Aslaksen. May I ask if your father-in-law is not going round the town buying up all the shares in the Baths?

Dr. Stockmann. Yes, he has been buying Baths shares today; but—

Aslaksen. It would have been more prudent to get someone else to do it—someone less nearly related to you.

Hovstad. And you should not have let your name appear in the affair. There was no need for anyone to know that the attack on the Baths came from you. You ought to have consulted me, Dr. Stockmann.

Dr. Stockmann (looks in front of him; then a light seems to dawn on him and he says in amazement.) Are such things conceivable? Are such things possible?

Aslaksen (with a smile). Evidently they are. But it is better to use a little finesse, you know.

Hovstad. And it is much better to have several persons in a thing of that sort; because the responsibility of each individual is lessened, when there are others with him.

Dr. Stockmann (composedly). Come to the point, gentlemen. What do you want?

Aslaksen. Perhaps Mr. Hovstad had better—

Hovstad. No, you tell him, Aslaksen.

Aslaksen. Well, the fact is that, now we know the bearings of the whole affair, we think we might venture to put the "People's Messenger" at your disposal.

Dr. Stockmann. Do you dare do that now? What about public opinion? Are you not afraid of a storm breaking upon our heads?

Hovstad. We will try to weather it.

Aslaksen. And you must be ready to go off quickly on a new tack, Doctor. As soon as your invective has done its work—

Dr. Stockmann. Do you mean, as soon as my father-in-law and I have got hold of the shares at a low figure?

Hovstad. Your reasons for wishing to get the control of the Baths are mainly scientific, I take it.

Dr. Stockmann. Of course; it was for scientific reasons that I persuaded the old "Badger" to stand in with me in the matter. So we will tinker at the conduit-pipes a little, and dig up a little bit of the shore, and it shan't cost the town a sixpence. That will be all right—eh?

Hovstad. I think so—if you have the "People's Messenger" behind you.

Aslaksen. The Press is a power in a free community. Doctor.

Dr. Stockmann. Quite so. And so is public opinion. And you, Mr. Aslaksen—I suppose you will be answerable for the Householders' Association?

Aslaksen. Yes, and for the Temperance Society. You may rely on that.

Dr. Stockmann. But, gentlemen—I really am ashamed to ask the question—but, what return do you—?

Hovstad. We should prefer to help you without any return whatever, believe me. But the "People's Messenger" is in rather a shaky condition; it doesn't go really well; and I should be very unwilling to suspend the paper now, when there is so much work to do here in the political way.

Dr. Stockmann. Quite so; that would be a great trial to such a friend of the people as you are. (Flares up.) But I am an enemy of the people, remember! (Walks about the room.) Where have I put my stick? Where the devil is my stick?

Hovstad. What's that?

Aslaksen. Surely you never mean—

Dr. Stockmann (standing still.) And suppose I don't give you a single penny of all I get out of it? Money is not very easy to get out of us rich folk, please to remember!

Hovstad. And you please to remember that this affair of the shares can be represented in two ways!

Dr. Stockmann. Yes, and you are just the man to do it. If I don't come to the rescue of the "People's Messenger," you will certainly take an evil view of the affair; you will hunt me down, I can well imagine—pursue me—try to throttle me as a dog does a hare.

Hovstad. It is a natural law; every animal must fight for its own livelihood.

Aslaksen. And get its food where it can, you know.

Dr. Stockmann (walking about the room). Then you go and look for yours in the gutter; because I am going to show you which is the strongest animal of us three! (Finds an umbrella and brandishes it above his head.) Ah, now—!

Hovstad. You are surely not going to use violence!

Aslaksen. Take care what you are doing with that umbrella.

Dr. Stockmann. Out of the window with you, Mr. Hovstad!

Hovstad (edging to the door). Are you quite mad!

Dr. Stockmann. Out of the window, Mr. Aslaksen! Jump, I tell you! You will have to do it, sooner or later.

Aslaksen (running round the writing-table). Moderation, Doctor—I am a delicate man—I can stand so little—(calls out) help, help!

(MRS. STOCKMANN, PETRA and HORSTER come in from the sitting-room.)

Mrs. Stockmann. Good gracious, Thomas! What is happening?

Dr. Stockmann (brandishing the umbrella). Jump out, I tell you! Out into the gutter!

Hovstad. An assault on an unoffending man! I call you to witness, Captain Horster. (Hurries out through the hall.)

Aslaksen (irresolutely). If only I knew the way about here—. (Steals out through the sitting-room.)

Mrs. Stockmann (holding her husband back). Control yourself, Thomas!

Dr. Stockmann (throwing down the umbrella). Upon my soul, they have escaped after all.

Mrs. Stockmann. What did they want you to do?

Dr. Stockmann. I will tell you later on; I have something else to think about now. (Goes to the table and writes something on a calling-card.) Look there, Katherine; what is written there?

Mrs. Stockmann. Three big Noes; what does that mean.

Dr. Stockmann. I will tell you that too, later on. (Holds out the card to Petra.) There, Petra; tell sooty-face to run over to the "Badger's" with that, as quick as she can. Hurry up! (PETRA takes the card and goes out to the hall.)

Dr. Stockmann. Well, I think I have had a visit from every one of the devil's messengers to-day! But now I am going to sharpen my pen till they can feel its point; I shall dip it in venom and gall; I shall hurl my inkpot at their heads!

Mrs. Stockmann. Yes, but we are going away, you know, Thomas.

(PETRA comes back.)

Dr. Stockmann. Well?

Petra. She has gone with it.

Dr. Stockmann. Good.—Going away, did you say? No, I'll be hanged if we are going away! We are going to stay where we are, Katherine!

Petra. Stay here?

Mrs. Stockmann. Here, in the town?

Dr. Stockmann. Yes, here. This is the field of battle—this is where the fight will be. This is where I shall triumph! As soon as I have had my trousers sewn up I shall go out and look for another house. We must have a roof over our heads for the winter.

Horster. That you shall have in my house.

Dr. Stockmann. Can I?

Horsier. Yes, quite well. I have plenty of room, and I am almost never at home.

Mrs. Stockmann. How good of you, Captain Horster!

Petra. Thank you!

Dr. Stockmann (grasping his hand). Thank you, thank you! That is one trouble over! Now I can set to work in earnest at once. There is an endless amount of things to look through here, Katherine! Luckily I shall have all my time at my disposal; because I have been dismissed from the Baths, you know.

Mrs. Stockmann (with a sigh). Oh yes, I expected that.

Dr. Stockmann. And they want to take my practice away from me too. Let them! I have got the poor people to fall back upon, anyway—those that don't pay anything; and, after all, they need me most, too. But, by Jove, they will have to listen to me; I shall preach to them in season and out of season, as it says somewhere.

Mrs. Stockmann. But, dear Thomas, I should have thought events had showed you what use it is to preach.

Dr. Stockmann. You are really ridiculous, Katherine. Do you want me to let myself be beaten off the field by public opinion and the compact majority and all that devilry? No, thank you! And what I want to do is so simple and clear and straightforward. I only want to drum into the heads of these curs the fact that the liberals are the most insidious enemies of freedom—that party programmes strangle every young and vigorous truth—that considerations of expediency turn morality and justice upside down—and that they will end by making life here unbearable. Don't you think, Captain Horster, that I ought to be able to make people understand that?

Horster. Very likely; I don't know much about such things myself.

Dr. Stockmann. Well, look here—I will explain! It is the party leaders that must be exterminated. A party leader is like a wolf, you see—like a voracious wolf. He requires a certain number of smaller victims to prey upon every year, if he is to live. Just look at Hovstad and Aslaksen! How many smaller victims have they not put an end to—or at any rate maimed and mangled until they are fit for nothing except to be householders or subscribers to the "People's Messenger"! (Sits down on the edge of the table.) Come here, Katherine—look how beautifully the sun shines to-day! And this lovely spring air I am drinking in!

Mrs. Stockmann. Yes, if only we could live on sunshine and spring air, Thomas.

Dr. Stockmann. Oh, you will have to pinch and save a bit—then we shall get along. That gives me very little concern. What is much worse is, that I know of no one who is liberal-minded and high-minded enough to venture to take up my work after me.

Petra. Don't think about that, father; you have plenty of time before you.—Hello, here are the boys already!

(EJLIF and MORTEN come in from the sitting-room.)

Mrs. Stockmann. Have you got a holiday?

Morten. No; but we were fighting with the other boys between lessons—

Ejlif. That isn't true; it was the other boys were fighting with us.

Morten. Well, and then Mr. Rorlund said we had better stay at home for a day or two.

Dr. Stockmann (snapping his fingers and getting up from the table). I have it! I have it, by Jove! You shall never set foot in the school again!

The Boys. No more school!

Mrs. Stockmann. But, Thomas—

Dr. Stockmann. Never, I say. I will educate you myself; that is to say, you shan't learn a blessed thing—

Morten. Hooray!

Dr. Stockmann. —but I will make liberal-minded and high-minded men of you. You must help me with that, Petra.

Petra, Yes, father, you may be sure I will.

Dr. Stockmann. And my school shall be in the room where they insulted me and called me an enemy of the people. But we are too few as we are; I must have at least twelve boys to begin with.

Mrs. Stockmann. You will certainly never get them in this town.

Dr. Stockmann. We shall. (To the boys.) Don't you know any street urchins—regular ragamuffins—?

Morten. Yes, father, I know lots!

Dr. Stockmann. That's capital! Bring me some specimens of them. I am going to experiment with curs, just for once; there may be some exceptional heads among them.

Morten. And what are we going to do, when you have made liberal-minded and high-minded men of us?

Dr. Stockmann. Then you shall drive all the wolves out of the country, my boys!

(EJLIF looks rather doubtful about it; MORTEN jumps about crying "Hurrah!")

Mrs. Stockmann. Let us hope it won't be the wolves that will drive you out of the country, Thomas.

Dr. Stockmann. Are you out of your mind, Katherine? Drive me out! Now—when I am the strongest man in the town!

Mrs. Stockmann. The strongest—now?

Dr. Stockmann. Yes, and I will go so far as to say that now I am the strongest man in the whole world.

Morten. I say!

Dr. Stockmann (lowering his voice). Hush! You mustn't say anything about it yet; but I have made a great discovery.

Mrs. Stockmann. Another one?

Dr. Stockmann. Yes. (Gathers them round him, and says confidentially:) It is this, let me tell you—that the strongest man in the world is he who stands most alone.

Mrs. Stockmann (smiling and shaking her head). Oh, Thomas, Thomas!

Petra (encouragingly, as she grasps her father's hands). Father!